# ROSE ELLIOT'S

# OXFAM

# VEGETARIAN COOKING FOR CHILDREN

D0242640

# ROSE ELLIOT'S

# OXFAM

# VEGETARIAN COOKING FOR CHILDREN

VERMILION
LONDON

First published 1995

1 3 5 7 9 10 8 6 4 2

First published in the United Kingdom in 1995 by
Vermilion, an imprint of Ebury Press
Random House, 20 Vauxhall Bridge Road, London, SW1V 2SA

Random House Australia (Pty) Limited
20 Alfred Street, Milsons Point, Sydney,
New South Wales 2061, Australia

Random House New Zealand Limited
18 Poland Road, Glenfield,
Auckland 10, New Zealand

Random House South Africa (Pty) Limited
PO Box 337, Bergvlei, South Africa

Random House UK Limited Reg. No. 954009

A CIP catalogue record for this book is available from the British Library.

Edited by Jane Middleton
Designed by Roger Walker/Graham Harmer
Photographed and styled by Michelle Garrett

ISBN 0 09 180816 2

Printed and bound in Great Britain by
Mackays of Chatham plc, Kent

# CONTENTS

# ABOUT OXFAM

This is a book about good food from around the world, and the enjoyment of cooking and eating with friends and family. The recipes were sent in by Oxfam supporters, volunteers in Oxfam shops, Oxfam staff in countries all over the world, and children and adults who had heard we were looking for good vegetarian recipes. We are very grateful to the celebrities who have contributed to this book.

Oxfam is very pleased to be able to work with Rose Elliot again. Rose has been a supporter of Oxfam in many ways for a long time and this is her third book for Oxfam. In 1992 she compiled the *Oxfam Vegetarian Cookbook*, which has been very successful in raising funds for Oxfam's work and continues to provide readers with exciting ideas for cooking.

Oxfam UK and Ireland is one of a family of Oxfam organizations around the world. You can find details of all national Oxfams at the end of this section.

# OXFAM AT WORK

## Food: enough for everyone?

The world produces more than enough food for everyone but tonight 700 million people – one sixth of the planet's population – will go to bed hungry. And despite massive increases in agricultural production, poor people today have less to eat than they did 40 years ago.

Rapid population growth is sometimes blamed for hunger and malnutrition. Yet since 1950 world production of grain has increased faster than population growth. Floods, drought and other natural disasters can also contribute to food shortages. But what really makes people vulnerable is poverty. People go hungry because they do not have enough money to buy food or enough land on which to grow it. When you have very little, there is no cushion against disaster.

Since colonial times, farmers in economically developing countries have grown crops for export to industrialized countries – tea, coffee, cotton, bananas – sometimes at the expense of food crops for their own families. The colonial era has ended but dependence on cash crops has continued, and many countries face a dilemma. Should they raise crops for export to pay off foreign debt or food crops to feed their growing populations?

In the long term, hunger cannot be solved by farmers or food aid alone but by changing the policies that cause poverty and create this dilemma.

## Organic gardening in Bangladesh

The Community Development Association (CDA) in Bangladesh is a project supported by Oxfam UK and Ireland which helps people in many ways. One of them is growing better crops without chemicals. CDA promotes what gardeners in this country would call organic methods, which means growing crops using natural products and avoiding all forms of chemical fertilizers and pesticides. Instead of using chemical fertilizers people make compost, and CDA advises group members to make use of locally available materials. Fifteen-year-old Mossammat Monowara Khatoun makes compost with cow dung, weeds and all kinds of rubbish and litter. She says, 'Chemical fertilizers ruin the land by reducing the fertility of the soil, and the soil retains less water. They also cost money, whereas compost can be made at home.'

Monowara uses the compost in her vegetable garden to grow a wide range of vegetables – onions, aubergines, cauliflower and cabbage – and also to cultivate wheat. Improved yields enable Monowara to earn more from her garden and contribute to her family's income. 'I paid for my education and bought new clothes. Now I also keep chickens and ducks, which I bought with the profit,' she explains.

Simple ideas, appropriate technology, practical results: all in all, it's a model of good development.

## Food aid

When drought, conflict, or some other disaster prevents people from growing enough food for their own needs, it may be necessary to provide food aid. Oxfam and other aid agencies have long experience of this. We try to buy food as near as possible to those who need it. This means people get food they are used to eating, and it encourages local production. Food brought in from outside the region can have the effect of pushing down prices and discouraging local production, resulting in a spiral of dependency.

When the crisis is over – when the rains fall, or when the conflict is over and people can return home – it is important to help people to start growing their own crops again. Seeds, tools and draught animals may all have to be provided, as well as enough food to eat until the first crop is harvested. This kind of help, which Oxfam often provides, is just as important as food aid itself.

## Food trade

Most small-scale farmers in economically developing countries grow food for themselves and their families. But they also need cash to pay for things they can't grow – salt, soap, clothes, school fees, taxes. They earn cash by selling crops. This may be a crop they grow for their own use, like rice, or it may be grown only for export to the richer countries of the developed world – a crop such as coffee, tea or cocoa. Their small harvests leave no cushion if the crops fail, if local traders reduce the price they pay, or if world commodity prices fall. As a result, many peasant farmers get into debt, and some have to abandon their land. They may drift to overcrowded cities in search of work.

## How Oxfam helps

Oxfam United Kingdom and Ireland works with poor people and their organizations in over 70 countries. Oxfam believes that all people have basic rights: to earn a living and to have food, shelter, health care and education. Oxfam provides relief in emergencies and gives long-term support to people struggling to build a better life for themselves and their families.

## Oxfam and food

All over the world people are working together to do something about the causes of poverty and hunger. Communities and groups are identifying and finding 'home-grown' solutions to such problems as how to raise more and better-quality food, how to market and store it, and how to improve health by growing and eating the right kinds of food.

Oxfam supports these grassroots initiatives by providing funding, training, or both, to meet present needs while safeguarding the environment for future generations – a process known as sustainable development.

## Relief and development

In addition to relief work in emergencies, Oxfam UK and Ireland supports some 3,000 development projects in over 70 countries every year. Some of them directly help people to grow more food. All of them tackle poverty. In 1993–4 Oxfam spent £73.7m on its overseas programme.

## Fair trade

Oxfam wants to see Fair Trade: small-scale producers and farmers getting a decent price for their products. Oxfam's Bridge programme buys crafts and foods from producers in economically developing countries on Fair Trade terms. Bridge staff provide advice and training on design, marketing and other practical matters. In 1993–4 Bridge sales were £11.6m.

Oxfam also works to persuade more people to buy fairly traded products, both in Oxfam shops and in supermarkets. One of the most successful products is Cafédirect coffee, bought at a fair price from small farmers in Latin America and Africa. José Rivera Campoverde, a coffee grower from Peru, describes the benefits: 'Before we became involved in selling to Cafédirect, most of us could not afford medical treatment,' explains José. 'The higher price we get when we sell coffee to Cafédirect means that now our co-operative can afford to pay a doctor who will give treatment to our members. For myself, the price difference has meant I can afford more food for my family and send my children to school properly equipped with pens and notebooks for the first time.'

Many of Oxfam's 850 shops in the UK bring Fair Trade food to the high street. Oxfam shops are run by volunteers – 30,000 in total.

## Advocacy

Oxfam also works at an international level. Along with other aid agencies and other members of the international Oxfam family, it lobbies governments and international organizations to adopt policies that help rather than hinder poor people's efforts to break out of the cycle of poverty and hunger. Oxfam staff work to understand the causes of poverty and hunger. Their conclusions, based on their work with poor people, lead to recommendations about the policies of governments and the international organizations – European Union, United Nations, International Monetary Fund and World Bank – in which the governments of the rich countries are influential. Oxfam also works with its partners around the world to help them influence the policy of their governments.

## How you can help

You can help Oxfam's emergency, development, research and advocacy work by making a donation. There are schemes that enable supporters to follow the work of specific development projects. To find out more, ring 01865 312603.

You can buy Bridge goods in 625 Oxfam shops in the UK and through Oxfam's mail-order catalogue. Look out, too, for products carrying the Fair Trade mark, which helps shoppers identify food products, such as coffee, tea and chocolate, that give a better deal to producers in economically developing countries. They are available in Oxfam shops and many supermarkets. If you would like a copy of the mail-order catalogue, ring 01865 245011.

You can recycle your unwanted possessions by taking them into your local Oxfam shop. While there, you might want to offer some of their other goods a second life! And if you have any time to spare, you could volunteer to help in the shop.

You can support Oxfam's advocacy work by joining the Oxfam Campaigning Network. We keep you informed about the issues that affect the world's poor and tell you about effective actions you could take to support Oxfam's advocacy work, both on the wider issues and in support of specific communities like the banana growers of the Caribbean. If you'd like to know more, phone 01865 312603.

**To find out more about Oxfam write to us:**

In England:
OXFAM, 274 Banbury Road, Oxford OX2 7DZ

In Ireland:
OXFAM, 19 Clanwilliam Terrace, Dublin 2

In Northern Ireland:
OXFAM, 52–4 Dublin Road, Belfast BT2 7HN

In Scotland:
OXFAM, 5th floor, Fleming House, 134 Renfrew St, Glasgow G3 6ST

In Wales:
OXFAM, 46–8 Station Road, Llanishen, Cardiff CF4 5LU

In Australia:
Community Aid Abroad, 156 George St, Fitzroy, Victoria 3065

In Belgium:
OXFAM Belgique, 39 rue du Conseil, Bruxelles 1050

In Canada:
OXFAM Canada, 294 Albert St, Suite 300, Ottawa, Ontario K1P 6E6

In Hong Kong:
OXFAM Hong Kong, Ground floor 3B, June Garden, 28 Tung Chau St,
Tai Kok Tsui, Kowloon

In New Zealand:
OXFAM New Zealand, Room 101 La Gonda House, 203 Karangahape Rd,
Auckland 1

In Quebec:
OXFAM Quebec, 2330 rue Notre-Dame Ouest, Bureau 200, Montreal,
Quebec H3J 1N4

In the USA:
OXFAM America, 25 West Street, Boston, MA 0211-1206

In the Netherlands:
NOVIB, Amaliastraat 7, 2514 JC, The Hague

# INTRODUCTION

Cooking for children has its own special pleasures and challenges. Most children have strong likes and dislikes, time for cooking is often limited and there may be financial constraints, too. Yet when we cook for – or with – children we are helping them to form eating habits and attitudes to food that will influence their tastes and well-being far into the future, perhaps for a lifetime. An important and worthwhile task indeed, and one that can be fulfilling and fun too.

I think it is the element of fun, as well as love and joy, which came across most in the recipes we received for this book from Oxfam friends and volunteers. We asked for vegetarian or vegan recipes that were popular with children. We wanted to produce a book that would be useful to the growing number of people cooking for vegetarian children. As with our previous book, the *Oxfam Vegetarian Cookbook*, the response was immediate and enthusiastic, and we are very grateful to everyone who contributed. The majority of recipes in this book are for adults to make for children but there are also a number of recipes – some of them contributed by children – that they can make for themselves, with varying amounts of help as necessary. Hands-on experience in the kitchen from an early age is one of the best ways of encouraging a love of food and cooking and something which I feel is increasingly important for children now that cookery is no longer part of the regular school curriculum.

Recent opinion polls have shown an increasing trend away from meat towards vegetarianism, with children and young people in the vanguard. Further research has revealed that the most frequently quoted reason for giving up meat is respect for animals: if you love animals, why kill and eat them? There is also concern about ecological issues and the impact that the intensive rearing of animals for meat has upon the environment globally. Issues that concern children are the destruction of the rainforest to provide grazing land for meat-producing animals, the pollution of soils, rivers and lakes with nitrates, pesticides and growth hormones from manure, and the threat to entire marine ecosystems from over-fishing at sea. They see becoming vegetarian as a powerful and positive step that they can take to improve conditions.

This idealism is admirable but can a vegetarian or vegan diet supply all the essential nutrients? The answer is yes, if it is based on a variety of foods and includes whole grains, pulses, nuts and seeds, and fruit and vegetables – as the table on page 13 shows (devised by Dr Michael Klaper, one of America's foremost experts on vegetarian nutrition). This table is in fact vegan; if you are including eggs, milk and cheese in your diet you will find it even easier to consume all the nutrients you need. However, I would like to comment on the nutrients people worry about most when they, or their child, become vegetarian.

Top of the list, not surprisingly, comes protein. In practice, however, for most of the Western world it simply isn't a problem; neither is it necessary to worry about 'complementary proteins' or 'protein balancing'. In 1993 the authoritative and respected American Dietetic Association stated: 'Plant sources of protein alone can provide adequate amounts of the essential and non-essential amino acids, assuming that dietary protein sources from plants are reasonably varied and that caloric intake is sufficient to meet energy needs. Whole grains, legumes, vegetables, seeds and nuts all contain essential and non-essential amino acids. Conscious combining of these foods within a given meal, as the complementary protein dictum suggests, is unnecessary. Additionally, soya protein has been shown to be nutritionally equivalent in protein value to proteins of animal origin and, thus, can serve as the sole source of protein intake if desired.'

Other nutrients that sometimes cause concern are the B vitamins, vitamin D, iron and – strangely, since there is virtually none in meat – calcium. Most of the B vitamins present no problems for either vegetarians or vegans, although vegans do need to watch their intake of riboflavin,which is found in dairy produce. Useful sources for vegans are almonds, quinoa, millet, wheatgerm, barley, sesame and pumpkin seeds, hummus, dried fruit and soya beans. Some breakfast cereals are fortified with riboflavin and a 30 g (1 oz) serving can provide a quarter of the recommended daily intake. Vegetarians can obtain sufficient B12 from dairy produce, and vegans by eating any of the increasing range of foods enriched with this vitamin, such as some soya milks, yeast extract, most breakfast cereals and textured vegetable proteins. Vitamin D is not a problem either, although supplements may be advisable for people of Asian origin living in northerly countries and infants between six months and three years old, because of the depletion of vitamin D supplies needed in the process of bone formation. It is often included in multi-vitamin preparations, so you don't need to seek it out specially but if you do, make sure you're not getting it in any other supplement you're taking, as it is toxic when taken in excess.

Iron deficiency is one of the most common problems in the British diet but scientific studies have shown that vegetarians and vegans are no more likely to suffer from this than meat eaters. Good sources of iron in the vegetarian diet include pumpkin, sunflower and sesame seeds; pistachio nuts, almonds, cashew nuts, peanuts and peanut butter; hummus; cocoa, soya flour, fortified breakfast cereals such as cornflakes, molasses, quinoa, tofu, soya beans, red kidney beans, baked beans, oats, wheat and wheatgerm; dried apricots and peaches.

Getting enough calcium isn't difficult in either a well-balanced vegetarian or vegan diet. Vegetarians get calcium from milk and cheese and, although vegans don't eat these, strangely there isn't evidence of calcium deficiency in their diet. Apparently, although they consume less calcium their bodies use and store it far more efficiently than meat eaters.

So nutritionally there really isn't a problem and I think it is a pity that people so often dwell on the possible deficiencies of a vegetarian diet instead of the many advantages. For instance, research has shown that vegetarians and vegans are five times less likely to be admitted to hospitals than meat eaters and there is now overwhelming evidence that a vegetarian diet can significantly reduce the incidence of heart disease, cancers, hypertension, diabetes, osteoporosis and many other afflictions. It seems that it is the diet as a whole rather than any one factor that is protective and beneficial; and there are now thousands of children, raised as vegetarians from birth or converted at a young age, who are radiant examples of the health-giving, vitalizing and joyful qualities of this way of eating.

## HOW TO MEET DAILY NUTRITIONAL REQUIREMENTS ON A VEGETARIAN/VEGAN DIET

| Food group | What it provides | Some examples | How often to eat |
|---|---|---|---|
| whole grains and potatoes | energy, protein, oils, vitamins, fibre | brown rice, corn, millet, barley, bulgur, buckwheat, oats, muesli, bread, pasta, flour | 2–4 100g (4 oz) servings daily |
| pulses | protein, oils | green peas, lentils, chick peas, kidney beans, baked beans, soya products | 1–2 100g (4 oz) servings daily |
| green and yellow vegetables | vitamins, minerals, protein | broccoli, Brussels sprouts, spinach, cabbage, carrots, marrow, sweet potatoes, pumpkins, parsnips | 1–3 100g (4 oz) servings daily |
| nuts and seeds | energy, protein, oils, calcium, trace minerals | almonds, pumpkin seeds, walnuts, peanuts, sesame seeds, nut butters, tahini, sunflower seeds | 1–3 25g (1 oz) daily |
| fruit | energy, vitamins, minerals | all kinds | 3–6 pieces daily |
| vitamin and mineral foods | trace minerals and vitamin $B_{12}$ | (a) sea vegetables (b) $B_{12}$-fortified foods such as soya milk, TVP and breakfast cereals | 1 serving of (a) and (b) 3 times a week |

# RECIPE NOTES

Quantities are given in metric and Imperial measures. Follow one set of measurements only, not a combination, because they are not interchangeable.

All spoon measurements are level.

It is recommended that you use free-range eggs.

# SNACKS, SALADS & SOUPS

# EASY CHEESE DIP WITH RAINBOW VEGETABLES

*Serves 1–2*

*All my kids have loved this and I encouraged them to make it themselves as soon as they were old enough – it makes a nutritious snack for when they return home ravenous from school. It's also a good way to encourage them to eat raw vegetables - let them choose their favourites, then serve the dip surrounded with them or put them into a little basket and serve the dip separately. Good vegetables to use are radishes, cherry tomatoes, spears of cucumber, sticks of carrot or celery, cauliflower or broccoli florets, spring onions, baby sweetcorn and a few sprigs of fresh mint or parsley. Slivers of apples are also popular.*

40 g (1$^{1}/_{2}$ oz) softened butter or margarine
150 g (5 oz) cheese, quite finely grated
6 tablespoons milk
a pinch of grated nutmeg or chilli powder
freshly ground black pepper
a selection of vegetables (see above)

Put the butter or margarine into a small bowl and beat with a wooden spoon until it is well softened. Then beat in the grated cheese a little at a time, adding the milk, too, bit by bit, so that you end up with a soft, creamy mixture. Add nutmeg or chilli and black pepper to taste. Put the mixture into a small serving bowl or heap it on to 1 or 2 individual plates. Prepare the vegetables and either put them into a basket or on a serving plate, or arrange them around the pile of dip on the individual plates.

*Rose Elliot*

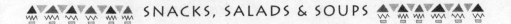
# HUMMUS

*Serves 4*

*Throughout the Middle East you'll find countless variations on hummus, a simple mixture of puréed chick peas and tahini (sesame seed paste). This version comes from Lebanon.*

425 g (15 oz) can of chick peas
4 tablespoons tahini
3 tablespoons lemon juice
1 large garlic clove, crushed
$\frac{1}{4}$ teaspoon ground cumin
salt
chopped fresh parsley and olive oil, to garnish (optional)

Drain the chick peas, reserving the liquid and a few peas. Place the remaining chick peas in a food processor or blender. Add the tahini, lemon juice, garlic, cumin and 4 tablespoons of the reserved liquid. Process until the mixture is smooth and has the consistency of soured cream, adding more liquid if necessary. Season to taste with salt.

Spread the hummus on a rimmed plate. Garnish with the reserved whole beans and with chopped parsley, if using. Or, if you wish, make several indentations in the hummus with the back of a spoon and fill them with olive oil.

*Nisrine Naaman, Oxfam, Lebanon*

Eat well.
Bon appétit.
Sahtein. (Lebanon)

# HUMMUS CROSTINI

*Serves 2–4*

*Crostini are great with other toppings, such as thick slices of tomato and grated cheese flashed quickly under the grill to melt the cheese.*

4 thick slices of French bread
1 garlic clove, peeled and cut in half
1 tablespoon olive oil
about 4 tablespoons hummus (see page 17)
cucumber sticks and lemon wedges, to serve

Toast the bread on both sides until golden on the outside but still soft in the centre. Rub one side of each piece of toast with the cut garlic clove, then drizzle over the olive oil and top with the hummus. Serve at once, with cucumber sticks and lemon wedges.

*Valerie Barrett*

# EGGY FRIES

*Serves 1*

2 eggs
salt and freshly ground black pepper
1 large, fairly thick slice of bread
butter or oil for frying

Break the eggs into a shallow bowl and whisk them together with salt and pepper to taste. Cut the bread in half and dip it into the eggs. Heat a little butter or oil in a frying pan and fry the bread on both sides until golden brown. Serve straight away.

*Leonn Seymour, Buckingham*

# BANANA CHEESE

*Serves 2*

*This is an unusual combination but a delicious snack. It is filling, nutritious and quick and easy to make. I just love it!*

2 large slices of bread (brown or white)
1 large banana, sliced
75 g (3 oz) Cheddar cheese, thinly sliced

Toast the bread on one side. Arrange the sliced banana over the untoasted side of the bread and place the cheese on top. Grill until the cheese is bubbling, about 2 minutes.

*Jane Allan (aged 11$^1/_2$ ), Forres, Moray*

# SPROUTING TOASTIES

*Serves 1*

1 slice of bread
a little butter
yeast extract or tomato sauce
25 g (1 oz) beansprouts
25 g (1 oz) cheese, grated (Cheddar works well)

Toast the bread lightly on both sides, then butter it and spread with yeast extract or tomato sauce. Sprinkle the beansprouts on top in a thin layer and then cover with the cheese. Put under the grill until the cheese has melted.

*Mrs M. L. Miller, Compton, Wolverhampton*

# CROQUE MONSIEUR JARVISSE

*Serves 1*

*This is something I invented while living in digs in Shepherds Bush near BBC Television Centre. I had just started working on TV and was cold, poor and hungry, with not many ingredients but a landlady who hoarded jars of wonderful things such as sun-dried tomatoes.*

2 thick slices of bread
a little butter and tomato purée
1 sun-dried tomato, chopped
25 g (1 oz) mature Cheddar cheese, grated
freshly ground black pepper

Toast the bread on one side, then butter the untoasted side and spread with tomato purée. Sprinkle the sun-dried tomato over the top and cover with the grated cheese. Replace under the grill and cook on low for a few minutes, then turn up high for a golden brown experience. Grind black pepper over and enjoy!

*Chris Jarvis*

# LEE'S QUICK PIZZA

*Serves 1*

oil or butter for frying
$1/4$ onion, finely chopped
1 slice of bread
$1/2$ tomato, sliced
15 g ($1/2$ oz) cheese, grated
salt and freshly ground black pepper

Heat a little oil or butter in a small pan and fry the onion until soft. Toast the bread on one side, then turn it over and put the slices of tomato on top. Arrange the onion over the tomato and sprinkle the grated cheese over that. Season and grill slowly until the cheese is melted and beginning to brown.

*Lee Donovan, London*

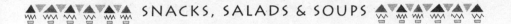 

# DEVILLED BANANAS

*Serves 4*

4 large slices of bread
2 bananas
salt
a squeeze of lemon juice
chopped fresh parsley, to garnish

*For the devilled butter*
75 g (3 oz) softened butter
a large pinch each of cayenne pepper,
curry powder and ground ginger

Beat together all the ingredients for the devilled butter until thoroughly combined. Toast the bread and cut each slice in half. Peel the bananas and cut them in half crossways, then cut them in half again lengthways and trim to an even length that will fit the toast. Spread some of the devilled butter on the toast and keep warm.

Dot the remaining devilled butter over the bananas and place under the grill until heated through. Place the bananas on the toast and sprinkle with a little salt and lemon juice. Garnish with parsley and serve.

*Mrs Rhiannon Evans, Corwen, Clwyd*

There are lots of different varieties of banana, from
sweet dessert bananas to large cooking bananas
which contain more starch and are picked when
the flesh is still hard. The latter are the staple
food of people in parts of East Africa and
can be cooked just like potatoes.

# CHEESE-TOPPED SAVOURIES

*Serves 2*

15 g ($^1/_2$ oz) butter or 1 tablespoon olive oil
75 g (3 oz) mushrooms, sliced
2 large tomatoes, skinned and chopped
$^1/_2$ teaspoon mustard (optional)
salt and freshly ground black pepper
4 slices of bread, buttered
50 g (2 oz) Cheddar cheese, grated
a little milk
fresh parsley, to garnish

Melt the butter or oil in a frying pan, add the mushrooms and tomatoes and cook for 1 minute, until softened. Stir in the mustard, if using, and season to taste. Divide the mixture between 2 of the slices of bread and top with the remaining 2 slices, pressing them down well. Toast the sandwiches on both sides under a preheated grill until golden brown.

Mix the cheese to a sticky consistency with a little milk and spread it over the top of the sandwiches. Return to the grill and cook until the cheese is bubbling and beginning to run over the sides. Garnish with parsley and serve at once.

*Lucy Day, Horsham, West Sussex*

# BREAD PIZZAS

*Serves 4*

*This recipe is ideal for using up leftover bread. Other ingredients such as diced mush-rooms may be added to the topping.*

4 slices of bread
1 small jar of ragù sauce
1 medium onion, diced
3–4 tomatoes, diced
250 g (8 oz) cheese, grated
salt and freshly ground black pepper

Lightly toast the bread on one side, then turn it over and spread thinly with the sauce. Mix together all the remaining ingredients and spread on top. Grill until golden brown.

*Stefanie Bryl, Oxfam volunteer, Nottingham*

A typical British 11-year-old consumes 4 packets of crisps, 6 cans of soft drink, 7 bars of chocolate, 7 biscuits, 3 bags of chips and 7 cakes each week.

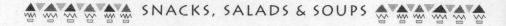 

# CHEESE ROLLS

*Serves 6*

125 g (4 oz) cheese, grated
50 g (2 oz) softened butter or margarine
a little milk
1–2 teaspoons mild mustard and/or 2–3 teaspoons
tomato ketchup, to taste
$\frac{1}{2}$ loaf of bread, thinly sliced

Put the cheese and butter or margarine in a bowl and mix with enough milk to make a spreadable consistency. Add mustard and/or tomato ketchup to taste, then spread the mixture on to each slice of bread and roll up like a Swiss roll. They can be frozen at this stage.

To cook the bread rolls, put them on a baking tray in an oven preheated to 200°C (400°F, Gas Mark 6) or place them under a preheated grill, turning to brown evenly. Spread with a little extra butter before serving, if you like.

*Stefanie Bryl, Nottingham*

'I get up, clean the plates and pans, help mother to cook, and feed the animals. I put rice on to boil and cut vegetables when I get home from school, then I fetch water and cook the rice.'

*Mosamat Roxana Begum, a ten-year-old girl on Hatiya island, Bangladesh*

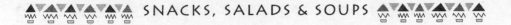 

# CASHEW NUT SPREAD

*Serves 4*

*Most children love nuts and this spread makes a change from bought peanut butter. It's a good sandwich filler or toast topper and is also nice spread on crackers. You can thin it down a bit with some milk and serve it as a dip for raw vegetables or bread-sticks.*

1 dessertspoon olive oil
1 small onion, very finely chopped
1 small garlic clove, crushed (optional)
65 g (2$\frac{1}{2}$ oz) toasted cashew nuts, ground
125 g (4 oz) silken tofu
1 tablespoon chopped fresh parsley
salt

Heat the oil in a small heavy frying pan and fry the onion and garlic, if using, until soft, stirring frequently. Transfer to a mixing bowl and stir in the nuts. Add all the remaining ingredients and mix together well, adding a little water if necessary to make a good spreading consistency. Taste and adjust the seasoning. This spread can be stored in a covered container in the fridge for up to 3 days.

*Judith Wills*

# LIVE MUESLI

*Serves 2*

*This recipe is similar to the original one developed by the famous Swiss physician, Max Bircher-Benner. Unlike packaged muesli, which usually contains too much sugar and is heavy and hard to digest, it contains a high proportion of fresh fruit. Kids love it. You can make it for yourself and for them. It can also be turned into a fine purée for a baby.*

$1/_2$ heaped tablespoon oatflakes
a handful of raisins or sultanas
fruit juice for soaking (optional)
1 apple or firm pear, grated or diced
1 small banana, finely chopped
2 teaspoons fresh orange juice
2 tablespoons sheep's or goat's milk yogurt or 2 tablespoons soya milk
1 teaspoon honey or blackstrap molasses (optional)
1 tablespoon chopped nuts or sunflower seeds
$1/_2$ teaspoon ground cinnamon or ginger

Soak the oatflakes and the raisins or sultanas overnight in a little water or fruit juice. In the morning, combine them with the apple or pear and banana, then add the orange juice to prevent the fruit browning and to aid digestion. Top with the yogurt or soya milk, then drizzle with the honey or molasses, if using. Sprinkle with the chopped nuts or sunflower seeds and the spices.

*Leslie Kenton*

'I prepare breakfast – it's a kind of porridge called *mingau de arroz*, made from rice and a sweet vegetable called *jerimun*. I sweep the floor, lay the table, and the family arrives for breakfast.'

*Margareth De Souza Brito, a 15-year-old schoolgirl in Maturuca village, North Brazil*

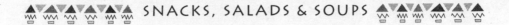 

# MOSIMANN'S MUESLI PANCAKES

*Serves 24*

*I created this recipe with health in mind and the flexibility to meet the demands of a hungry family, as it can be prepared the night before and is still something different and creative to enjoy in the morning. As a Swiss, I have tasted all sorts of muesli but nothing is quite like this and I love breakfast!*

60 g (2¹/₄ oz) medium oatflakes
1 large egg, beaten
150 ml (¹/₄ pint) milk
a pinch of salt
2 teaspoons baking powder
6 pieces of dried apricot, chopped
2 pieces of dried pear, chopped
2 tablespoons raisins
1 tablespoon chopped nuts
1 apple, grated
butter for greasing
icing sugar for dusting

Mix all the ingredients except the butter and icing sugar together and let the mixture rest for about 30–60 minutes for the oatflakes to swell. Heat a frying pan or griddle and grease with a little butter. Drop the batter in by the dessert-spoonful, about 3 at a time. Cook slowly for about 3 minutes, until the edges start to set, then turn over and cook the other side until lightly browned. Keep warm. Repeat until the mixture is finished. Serve immediately with a dusting of icing sugar.

*Anton Mosimann*

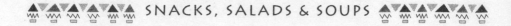 

# ULTIMATE COLESLAW

*Serves 4–6*

*This coleslaw has such a marvellous flavour and texture, it's hard to believe it's good for you as well!*

500 g (1 lb) white cabbage
250 g (8 oz) carrots, coarsely grated
125 g (4 oz) spring onions, chopped (white and green parts)
1 red apple, cored and finely chopped

*For the dressing*
125 ml (4 fl oz) olive oil
4 tablespoons grapeseed oil or mild vegetable oil
juice of 1 lemon
1 garlic clove, crushed
1 heaped tablespoon runny honey
1 teaspoon Dijon mustard
salt and freshly ground black pepper

Cut the cabbage into quarters, then cut out the thick core and finely shred the leaves with a sharp knife. Mix the cabbage, carrots, spring onions and apple together in a large bowl.

To make the dressing, simply process all the ingredients together in a blender or whisk them together in a bowl. Pour over the vegetables and toss until they are lightly coated in this delicious, golden dressing. Leave the coleslaw in the fridge for a few hours before serving to bring out all the flavours.

*Michael Barry*

'We used to sell a bundle of cabbages for
100 *rupiah* but the price has gone down to about 50
*rupiah* because so many people are growing them
now. We have to sell more, for less.'

*Korlina Kahilep, treasurer of a women's group
in West Sumba, Indonesia*

# CARROT AND RADISH SALAD

*Serves 2*

*White radish (mooli) can be found in large supermarkets, Indian and oriental stores. If you cannot find it, use another kind of radish.*

1 medium carrot, thinly sliced
250 g (8 oz) white radish, thinly sliced
1 tablespoon sesame oil
1 tablespoon rice wine vinegar or white wine vinegar
$1/4$ teaspoon soy sauce
$1/4$ teaspoon sugar
a pinch of cayenne pepper
salt

Put the carrot and radish slices into a salad bowl. Mix together all the other ingredients and pour them over the vegetables, stirring well to distribute evenly. Leave the salad to absorb the dressing for 1 hour before serving.

'I get up at about six o'clock and have breakfast – rice, vegetables, greens, and potatoes – which my sister cooks.'

*Maman, a 14-year-old boy living in Bandung, Indonesia*

29

# SPIDERMAN SALAD

Kids are meant to hate salads but, in my experience, what most very young children hate is not the salad but the texture, because the ingredients are not cut finely enough. I don't blame them. I don't like salads either unless they have real aesthetic variety – the contrasting colours of the vegetables, the way they are cut, and the presentation. I started my children on what my youngest calls 'Spiderman Salad'. He came up with that name one day when I was explaining to him that if you wanted to be strong, like Spiderman, you needed to eat lots of raw vegetables. These first salads are more like vegetable pâtés. You can chop or purée them (depending on the age of the child) in a food processor or with a hand-held blender. The secret is the binding ingredient, such as avocado, ground cashew nuts or puréed hard-boiled eggs. The great thing about these 'Spidermans' is that once they have been chopped or puréed they are highly concentrated. A dessertspoonful at a meal can give more nourishment than an adult side salad.

When you make any salad for yourself, put a little of it into a blender or food processor, including some dressing, add a spoonful of cashew nuts, avocado, the yolk of a hard-boiled egg, or even a little thick yogurt or tofu – something that will bind it together. Process briefly and season with vegetable bouillon powder and herbs, plus a little salt and maybe a drop or two of olive oil. The resulting 'Spiderman' salad is really a pâté, which can even be spread on crackers for older children.

*Leslie Kenton*

# FRUITY VEGETABLE SALAD

*Serves 6*

*The inclusion of fruit in a savoury salad generally makes it more appealing to children. Omit the nuts, or chop them very finely, if serving to very young children.*

1 tablespoon soy sauce
2 tablespoons orange juice
1 tablespoon smooth peanut butter
3 tablespoons vegetable oil
4 satsumas or 2 large seedless oranges
1 eating apple, cored and chopped
about $1/4$ small cucumber, finely shredded
1 large carrot, finely shredded
50 g (2 oz) sprouted beans of your choice or beansprouts
50 g (2 oz) salted peanuts

To make the dressing, whisk together the soy sauce, orange juice, peanut butter and oil. Peel the satsumas, if using, and separate into segments. If using oranges, remove all the peel and white pith, then chop into bite-sized pieces. Stir into the dressing. Mix the apple, cucumber and carrot into the dressing and orange mixture, then add the beansprouts and peanuts. Mix everything together well and serve immediately.

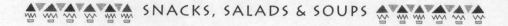 

# CREAMY TOMATO AND CARROT SOUP

*Serves 3–4*

*Children like this soup because of the slight sweetness from the carrots. For a variation you could throw in 50 g (2 oz) of animal pasta shapes before you add the milk: cook them in the soup for a few minutes until they are tender, then add the milk and a little more water if necessary.*

25 g (1 oz) butter or margarine
1 onion, chopped
250 g (8 oz) carrots, diced
400 g (13 oz) can of tomatoes
450 ml ($^3/_4$ pint) water
150–300 ml ($^1/_4$–$^1/_2$ pint) creamy milk
salt and freshly ground black pepper
fingers of hot buttered toast, perhaps with Marmite, to serve

Melt the butter or margarine in a saucepan, stir in the onion and carrots, then cover and cook gently for 10 minutes. Add the tomatoes and their juice to the pan, breaking them up with a spoon, then add the water. Cover and simmer for about 30 minutes, or until the carrots are very tender. Liquidize the soup and return it to the pan. Stir in enough milk to give the consistency you want, then season with salt and pepper. Reheat gently and serve with fingers of toast.

*Rose Elliot*

# MISO SOUP

*Serves 2*

*Soup forms a part of nearly every meal in Japan and miso soup is a favourite for breakfast. You can add dried seaweed, tofu, vegetables and fish to give colour and flavour to this recipe. Miso is made from soya beans that have been fermented, steamed and salted. It can be bought from Japanese shops.*

2 spring onions, green parts only, cut into 4 cm (1$^{1}/_{2}$ inch) lengths
125 g (4 oz) tofu, cut into small cubes
300 ml ($^{1}/_{2}$ pint) dashi (Japanese fish stock), or
1 vegetable stock cube mixed with 300 ml ($^{1}/_{2}$ pint) water
2 tablespoons red miso

Place the spring onions and tofu in 2 soup bowls. Bring the stock to the boil in a saucepan, then pour a little of it into a bowl and mix with the miso. Pour it back into the saucepan and stir well to combine with the rest of the stock, then ladle it into the soup bowls. Serve immediately.

*Jenny Ridgwell*

## DID YOU KNOW?

China only has 7 per cent of the world's cultivable land and yet it manages to feed 20 per cent of the world's population.

33

# CREAMY ONION SOUP

*Serves 4–6*

50 g (2 oz) butter
750 g (1½ lb) onions, thinly sliced
25 g (1 oz) fresh white breadcrumbs
600 ml (1 pint) milk
600 ml (1 pint) vegetable stock
salt and freshly ground black pepper
a few croûtons, to serve (optional)

Melt the butter in a large pan, add the onions, then cover and cook over a very low heat for 1 hour, making sure that the onions do not colour. Add the breadcrumbs, milk, stock and salt and pepper to taste. Bring to the boil, then reduce the heat, cover and simmer gently for 45 minutes. Purée the soup in a blender or food processor, then return to the pan and reheat gently. Adjust the seasoning and serve, sprinkled with croûtons if wished, or accompanied by crusty bread.

*Jane Middleton*

# CHEESE & EGGS

# EGGS IN A BLANKET

*Serves 2*

*A simple dish which children love. Serve it with fingers of hot toast.*

15 g ($^1/_2$ oz) butter or margarine
15 g ($^1/_2$ oz) plain flour
200 ml (7 fl oz) milk
2 tablespoons chopped fresh parsley
salt and freshly ground black pepper
3–4 hard-boiled eggs

Melt the butter or margarine in a pan, then stir in the flour. When it froths at the edges add the milk, stirring well. Continue to stir until the sauce thickens, then leave it over a very gentle heat for 7–10 minutes to cook the flour. Remove from the heat, add the parsley and season to taste.

Cut the eggs in half and place them, yolk-side down in a shallow casserole or on 2 warmed plates. Pour the sauce over the eggs to cover them completely and serve at once, with fingers of toast.

*Rose Elliot*

'I like eating and don't like the fact that there isn't enough food and clothes here.'

*Gakosa Yohanna, 9-year-old Rwandan refugee living in Kagenyi camp, Tanzania*

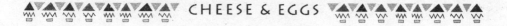 

# CHEESE FRITTERS

*Serves 4*

*Readers of some of my other cookery books will probably recognize this recipe. However, I have decided to include it here as it is perhaps my most popular recipe with children. The fritters are a little time-consuming to make but well worth the effort. They freeze excellently (after coating with crumbs) and can be cooked from frozen. A parsley sauce goes very well with them (see page 78), and also some frozen peas or cooked broccoli and Healthy Home-made Oven Chips (see page 113).*

600 ml (1 pint) milk
1 small onion, peeled and stuck with 2–3 cloves
1 bay leaf
125 g (4 oz) semolina
125–175 g (4–6 oz) Cheddar cheese, grated
1 teaspoon mustard powder
2–4 tablespoons chopped fresh parsley (optional)
salt and freshly ground black pepper
1 large egg and dried breadcrumbs for coating
groundnut oil for shallow-frying
lemon wedges, to serve

Put the milk in a large saucepan with the onion and bay leaf. Bring to the boil, then remove from the heat, cover and leave for 15 minutes or more to infuse. Remove the onion and bay leaf, then bring the milk back to the boil. Sprinkle the semolina on top, stirring. Continue to stir until the mixture is smooth, then leave it over a gentle heat until thick – about 5 minutes. Remove the pan from the heat and stir in the cheese, mustard and parsley, if using. Season well with salt and pepper, then press the mixture out on a plate or baking tray in a layer about 8 mm/$^3/_8$ inch thick. Leave for at least an hour, preferably overnight, to cool and firm up.

Cut the mixture into fingers or triangles and dip them in beaten egg and then in dried breadcrumbs. Shallow-fry them in hot oil on both sides until they are crisp. Drain on kitchen paper and serve as soon as possible, with lemon wedges.

*Rose Elliot*

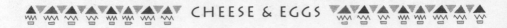 

# FRITTATA

*Serves 3*

*A frittata is easy to make and popular with most children – they even like eating it cold with their fingers! Choose their favourite vegetables, aiming for ones that take about the same time to cook. Here I've used peppers, courgettes, onions and spring onions but you could equally well include tomatoes, mushrooms or any other favourites. If you're using root vegetables such as potatoes or carrots, it's best to cook them first in boiling water until tender.*

3 tablespoons olive oil
1 onion, chopped
1 red pepper, chopped
1 yellow or orange pepper, chopped
1 large courgette, sliced
salt and freshly ground black pepper
3–4 spring onions, chopped
4 eggs, beaten
50 g (2oz) Gruyère or Cheddar cheese, grated
chopped fresh parsley, to garnish

Heat the oil in a frying pan, stir in the onion and peppers, then cover and cook gently for about 7 minutes or until all the vegetables are tender. Season with salt and pepper, then add the spring onions to the pan. Stir, then add the beaten eggs. Cook over a gentle heat for 4–5 minutes, or until the eggs have set underneath, then sprinkle with the cheese and put the pan under a hot grill for a few minutes until the egg has set completely. Remove from the heat and sprinkle with chopped parsley. Serve cut into wedges.

*Rose Elliot*

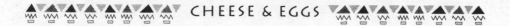 

# YOGURT OMELETTE

*Serves 2–3*

*Yogurt omelette should be served cold, either as a starter or as a light dinner with a green salad. You could cook the onions and garlic first if you prefer a milder flavour.*

4 eggs
2 teaspoons finely chopped fresh parsley
2 teaspoons finely chopped fresh mint
1 small onion, finely chopped
1–2 garlic cloves, finely chopped
1 tablespoon plain flour
a pinch of ground cinnamon
salt and freshly ground black pepper
vegetable oil for frying
50 g (2 oz) pine kernels
150 ml (¼ pint) thick Greek yogurt
a few lettuce leaves, chopped
2 tomatoes, sliced
½ cucumber, sliced

Mix together the eggs, parsley, mint, onion, garlic, flour, cinnamon and seasoning. Heat a thin layer of oil in a 15–18 cm (6–7 inch) omelette pan. Pour in 2 tablespoons of the egg mixture and spread evenly to form a thin omelette. Fry for 1–2 minutes until golden brown underneath, then turn and cook the other side. Remove from the pan and leave to cool. Repeat with the remaining mixture to make 6 omelettes.

Heat a little more oil in the pan and when it is very hot, fry the pine kernels until they are light brown. Remove from the pan and set aside.

Spread yogurt over each omelette and roll them up separately. Arrange the lettuce on serving plates and put the rolled omelettes on top, then surround with tomato and cucumber slices. Sprinkle the pine kernels over the omelettes.

*Lina Abu-Habib, Oxfam, Lebanon*

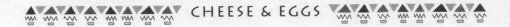 

# MELTING CHEESE AND BASIL PIE

*Serves 4*

4 eggs
600 ml (1 pint) milk
10 thin slices of bread (white or brown)
2 x 400 g (13 oz) cans of chopped tomatoes, partly drained
2 tablespoons chopped fresh parsley
2 tablespoons chopped fresh basil
salt and freshly ground black pepper
250 g (8 oz) mozzarella cheese (or Cheddar), thinly sliced

Preheat the oven to 200°C (400°F, Gas Mark 6). Grease a 750 ml (1$^1$/$_4$ pint) ovenproof dish. Beat together the eggs and milk, dip the bread into this mixture and arrange a third of the slices over the base of the dish. Pour a third of the tomatoes over the bread and sprinkle with some of the herbs. Season well and then top with some of the cheese. Continue layering in this way, finishing with tomato and herbs. Reserve a few slices of cheese.

Bake in the oven for 30 minutes, then arrange the remaining cheese on top and return to the oven until it has melted and browned. Serve with peas or any other green vegetable.

*Lucy Day, Horsham, West Sussex*

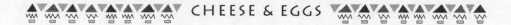 

# GREEN CHEESE PUFFS

*Serves 3–4*

*This is based on a recipe from Rose Elliot's* Simply Delicious *cookbook,* Cheese Puffs, *which I varied because I don't like walnuts but love spinach. For coeliacs, potato flour can be used instead of wheat flour.*

175 g (6 oz) Red Leicester cheese, finely grated
250 g (8 oz) fresh spinach, cooked, well drained and chopped
50 g (2 oz) plain flour
2 heaped tablespoons chopped fresh parsley
$^1/_2$ teaspoon paprika
2 eggs, separated
salt
sunflower oil for shallow-frying

Mix together the cheese, spinach, flour, parsley, paprika and egg yolks. Whisk the egg whites until stiff, then fold them gently into the mixture and season with salt. Shape the mixture into small balls. Heat a thin layer of sunflower oil in a frying pan and shallow-fry the spinach balls, a few at a time, for 4–6 minutes. Drain excess oil on kitchen paper and serve immediately.

*Megan Rosen-Webb, North Finchley, London*

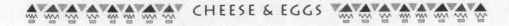 

# CHEESE FONDUE

*Serves 3*

125 g (4 oz) fresh breadcrumbs
300 ml ($\frac{1}{2}$ pint) milk
175 g (6 oz) Cheddar cheese, grated
2 eggs, beaten
salt and freshly ground black pepper

Preheat the oven to 200°C (400°F, Gas Mark 6). Butter an ovenproof dish. Put the breadcrumbs into the dish and pour the milk over them. Stir the cheese into the beaten eggs, season well and pour into the dish. Stir together and then bake in the oven for 20 minutes, until set and golden brown. Serve with sliced tomatoes and/or green beans.

*Betty McGhie, Wemyss Bay, Scotland*

Many people in the Third World cook over open fires, with three stones to support their cooking pot. This way of cooking damages the environment by using up precious wood supplies and is also harmful to people: cooking over a smoky fire can have the same effect as smoking 200 cigarettes a day. More efficient stoves can be made simply and cheaply, people just need to learn how.

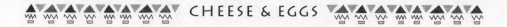 

# STUFFED EGGS

*Serves 4*

250 ml (8 fl oz) yogurt
1–2 teaspoons sugar
2.5 cm (1 inch) piece of cinnamon, crushed, or
1 teaspoon ground cinnamon
4 hard-boiled eggs, shelled
a handful of fresh parsley, finely chopped
1 small onion, grated
2–3 tablespoons olive oil
a pinch of paprika
salt and freshly ground black pepper
lettuce leaves

Put the yogurt in a bowl and add the sugar, mixing well. Sprinkle half the cinnamon on top. Cut the eggs in half lengthways, remove the yolks and put these into a bowl. Mash them with a fork and mix in the parsley and onion, then add enough olive oil to make a smooth mixture. Season with the remaining cinnamon, plus the paprika and salt and pepper.

Spoon some of the mixture into each egg white half and place them on a bed of lettuce leaves. Pour or spoon the yogurt-cinnamon dressing on top of the eggs and serve.

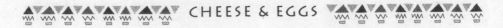 

# OMELETTE WITH BEANSPROUTS

*Serves 2*

*For this recipe you can use mung beansprouts or soy beansprouts.*

3 eggs
1 tablespoon milk
a dash of soy sauce
3 spring onions, finely chopped
125 g (4 oz) beansprouts
salt and freshly ground black pepper
1 tablespoon oil

Beat the eggs together in a bowl and then mix in the milk, soy sauce, spring onions, beansprouts and salt and pepper. Heat the oil in an omelette pan, pour in the egg mixture and make an omelette in the usual way. Serve immediately.

# EASY CAULIFLOWER CHEESE

*Serves 4*

1 large cauliflower, divided into florets
1 large can of macaroni cheese
75 g (3 oz) cheese, grated

Preheat the oven to 200°C (400°F, Gas Mark 6). Cook the cauliflower in boiling salted water until just tender, then drain thoroughly and place in a large oven-proof dish. Pour the macaroni cheese over, sprinkle with the grated cheese and bake in the oven for 20–25 minutes or until golden brown.

*Stefanie Bryl, Nottingham*

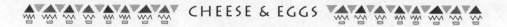 

# ROLLED OMELETTE WITH PEAS

*Serves 2*

*In Japan, this slightly sweet omelette is cooked in a special rectangular pan but you can use a round omelette pan instead. When the omelette is cooked it is rolled up and cut into small slices for a snack or packed lunch.*

3 eggs
100 ml (3$^{1}/_{2}$ fl oz) dashi (Japanese fish stock) or
1 vegetable stock cube mixed with 100 ml (3$^{1}/_{2}$ fl oz) water
1 teaspoon sugar
1 tablespoon light soy sauce
1 tablespoon cooked peas
oil for frying

Break the eggs into a bowl, add the stock, sugar and soy sauce and mix with a whisk or a fork. Add the peas. Heat a little oil in an omelette pan, then pour in enough egg mixture just to cover the base of the pan and cook until it begins to set.

Roll up the omelette to one side of the pan, using chopsticks or a fish slice. Add a little more oil to the pan, pour in more egg mixture and cook until set. Then roll up again towards the first roll. Repeat until all the egg mixture is used up.

Now press the omelette into shape. Remove it from the pan with a fish slice. Roll the omelette in a bamboo mat or a piece of kitchen foil and leave for 1 minute to set into shape. Cut the omelette into 2 cm ($^{3}/_{4}$ inch) slices and serve hot or cold.

*Jenny Ridgwell*

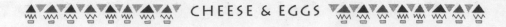 

# TOAD IN THE HOLE

*Serves 4*

*This is a traditional recipe, adapted for vegetarians. You could add chopped onion or herbs to the batter for a change. Serve with roast potatoes, a green vegetable and vegetarian gravy.*

125 g (4 oz) plain flour
$^1/_4$ teaspoon salt
2 large eggs, beaten
300 ml ($^1/_2$ pint) milk, or milk and water
a little vegetable oil
500 g (1 lb) vegetarian sausages (or Sosmix)

Preheat the oven to 220°C (425°F, Gas Mark 7). Sift the flour and salt into a bowl, make a well in the centre and add the beaten eggs. Stir in half the milk, gradually drawing in the flour. Beat vigorously until the mixture is smooth and bubbly, then stir in the rest of the milk. Set aside for 30 minutes.

Pour a little oil into a shallow ovenproof dish, add the sausages and cook in the oven until just browned but not cooked through. Pour the batter over the hot sausages and bake for 40–45 minutes, until well risen and golden brown.

*Joy Cook, Epping, Essex*

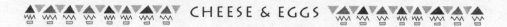 

# CHEESE AND ONION BREAD BAKE

*Serves 4*

*This is a perfect main-course dish for children – it's high in protein, vitamins and minerals and tastes delicious. It is also low-cost and dead easy to make, so it's ideal for parents too!*

1 tablespoon corn oil
1 large onion, finely chopped
$\frac{1}{2}$ teaspoon dried thyme
125 g (4 oz) Cheddar cheese, grated
75 g (3 oz) Parmesan cheese, freshly grated
1 dessertspoon chopped fresh chives
8 medium slices of wholemeal bread, crusts removed
3 eggs
500 ml (18 fl oz) skimmed milk
freshly ground black pepper

Preheat the oven to 190°C (375°F, Gas Mark 5). Brush a rectangular baking dish with a little of the oil. Heat the rest of the oil in a frying pan and cook the onion and thyme over a low-medium heat for about 15 minutes, stirring frequently, until the onion is very soft and just turning golden.

Mix together the cheeses and chives. Arrange half the bread in the baking dish to fit exactly. Cover with the onion mixture and half the cheese mixture, then cover with the remaining slices of bread and top with the rest of the cheese mixture. Whisk the eggs and milk together in a bowl and season with pepper. Pour this over the bread and cheese and bake for 20 minutes, or until puffed up and golden. Serve with a large mixed salad.

*Judith Wills*

# PERUVIAN POTATOES WITH .HARD-BOILED EGG

*Serves 4*

*Two versions of this recipe were collected by Grace's mother in Peru in 1994 and there are probably many more. Potatoes came from South America originally, and are eaten there a great deal – as are cheese and eggs. In the area around Juliaca, a town which lies at an altitude of about 16,000 ft, people have adapted this recipe to use an Andean grain called kaniwa, instead of bread made of wheat.*

625 g (1¹/₄ lb) potatoes
4 lettuce leaves
2 eggs, hard-boiled and thinly sliced
parsley, to garnish (optional)

*For the sauce*
25 g (1 oz) butter
50 g (2 oz) onion, finely chopped
6 ripe tomatoes, skinned, seeded and chopped
6 tablespoons double cream
¹/₂ teaspoon dried oregano
1 teaspoon chopped fresh coriander
a pinch of cayenne pepper
salt and freshly ground black pepper
50 g (2 oz) mozzarella cheese, grated

Boil the potatoes, peeled or unpeeled, until tender and cut them into 1 cm (¹/₂ inch) slices.

For the sauce, melt the butter in a pan, add the onion and cook until tender but not brown. Add the tomatoes and cook for about 5 minutes, until they have broken down slightly. Stir in the cream, herbs, cayenne and seasoning and heat gently, then add the cheese and cook just until it melts.

Put a lettuce leaf on each plate and place the sliced potatoes on top. Cover the potatoes with the sauce, and put slices of egg on top. Garnish with parsley if you have some.

*Grace Coles and Jenny Warr (aged 9),*
*Church Enstone, Oxfordshire*

# SAVOURY PASTRY DISHES

# BROCCOLI AND SWEETCORN FLAN

*Serves 4–6*

*I devised this recipe partly to encourage my daughter, Claire, to eat broccoli, which is one of the most nutritious vegetables. It's good served hot, with mashed or new potatoes and cooked carrots, or cold with salad.*

25 g (1 oz) butter or margarine
25 g (1 oz) plain flour
300 ml ($\frac{1}{2}$ pint) milk or soya milk
375 g/12 oz broccoli, divided into florets, stalks chopped
125 g (4 oz) Cheddar cheese, grated
salt and freshly ground black pepper
125 g (4 oz) frozen sweetcorn

*For the pastry*
175 g (6 oz) wholemeal flour
$\frac{1}{2}$ teaspoon salt
75 g (3 oz) margarine, butter or white vegetable fat

First make the pastry. Sift the flour into a large bowl and tip in the bran left in the sieve. Add the salt, then rub in the fat until the mixture looks like breadcrumbs. Add 2–3 tablespoons of cold water and mix to a dough. If there's time, chill the dough for 15–30 minutes.

Preheat the oven to 200°C (400°F, Gas Mark 6). Roll the pastry out on a lightly floured work surface and use to line a 20 cm (8 inch) flan tin, about 2.5 cm (1 inch) deep. Cover with greaseproof paper, weigh down with baking beans or rice, then bake for 10 minutes. Remove the paper and beans or rice and bake for a further 10 minutes until crisp. Remove from the oven.

Melt the butter in a pan, then stir in the flour. When it froths at the edges, add the milk, stirring well. Stir until the sauce thickens, then leave it over a very gentle heat for 7–10 minutes. Meanwhile, cook the broccoli in boiling water for 3–4 minutes or until just tender, then drain well. Stir two-thirds of the cheese into the sauce and season to taste. Gently stir the broccoli and sweetcorn into the sauce and check the seasoning. Spoon the mixture into the flan case, sprinkle with the rest of the cheese, then return it to the oven for 15–20 minutes, until lightly browned.

*Rose Elliot*

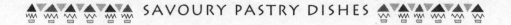 

# WHOLEWHEAT CHICK PEA PASTIES

*Makes 4*

*Children generally enjoy both making and eating pastry dishes, as I found when I demonstrated this dish in my daughter Claire's primary school. They ate up every crumb and for days afterwards children came up and told me they had later made the pasties themselves. Many 10-year-olds could manage this recipe with a bit of help.*

2 tablespoons olive oil
1 onion, chopped
250 g (8 oz) potato, cut into 5 mm ($^1/_4$ inch) dice
1 tablespoon ground coriander
1 teaspoon ground cumin
425 g (15 oz) can of chick peas, drained
salt and freshly ground black pepper

*For the pastry*
250 g (8 oz) wholemeal flour
$^1/_2$ teaspoon salt
125 g (4 oz) margarine, butter or white vegetable fat

Heat the oil in a saucepan, stir in the onion and potato, then cover and cook over a low heat for 10 minutes. Add the spices and cook for a minute, stirring. Remove from the heat and stir in the chick peas and seasoning. Leave to cool.

Sift the flour into a large bowl and tip in the bran left in the sieve (the reason for sifting the flour is to get air into it, not to remove the bran). Add the salt, then cut the fat into small cubes and rub it into the flour with your fingertips until the mixture looks like breadcrumbs. Now add enough cold water to make the mixture hold together in a dough; start with 3 tablespoons and add a little more after that if you need it. Wholemeal flour absorbs more water than white which is why you may need a drop more. Shape the dough into a ball and, if there's time, put it into a polythene bag and put it in the fridge to chill (this makes it easier to roll out). Meanwhile, heat the oven to 200°C (400°F, Gas Mark 6).

Divide the pastry into 4 equal pieces. Form each into a ball, then roll it out into a 15 cm (6 inch) circle – a small plate or saucer makes a good guide. Spoon a quarter of the filling into the centre of each circle, then fold the pastry up over the filling. Dampen the edges with a little water and pinch them together to seal. Make a couple of steam holes in the top, then put the pasties on to a baking sheet and bake for 20–25 minutes, until golden brown.

*Rose Elliot*

# BONAPARTE MUSHROOMS

*Serves 4*

*My wife's great-grandfather's name was Louis Clovis Bonaparte. I invented this recipe with her family in mind, hence the shape of the three-cornered hat.*

500 g (1 lb) puff pastry
250 g (8 oz) Brie cheese, cut into 1 cm ($^1/_2$ inch) cubes
14–16 mushrooms, about 4 cm ($1^1/_2$ inch) in diameter, stalks removed
1 egg, beaten with a drop of milk
chopped fresh chives or parsley, to garnish

*For the sauce*
250 g (8 oz) mushrooms, very finely chopped
1 onion, very finely chopped
a knob of butter
150 ml ($^1/_4$ pint) unsweetened white grape juice
salt and freshly ground black pepper
about 6 tablespoons double cream

Preheat the oven to 220°C (425°F, Gas Mark 7). Roll out the puff pastry to about 5 mm ($^1/_4$ inch) thick, then cut it into triangles with sides 15 cm (6 inch) long.

Place the cheese inside the mushroom caps and then place a single mushroom in the centre of each pastry triangle. Brush the pastry edges with the beaten egg, then bring the three corners of the triangle up over the top of the mushroom and pinch together to make a shape like a three-cornered hat. Press the sides together to seal. Decorate with the pastry trimmings – you could cut out your initials, or make long thin strips of pastry and tie one around each triangle in a bow. Brush the pastry all over with beaten egg, then place the parcels on a greased baking tray and bake in the centre of the oven for about 12 minutes. The cheese sometimes runs out of the corners on to the tray a little but that's OK.

To make the sauce, fry the chopped mushrooms and onion in the butter until tender but not browned. Add the grape juice and salt and pepper to taste. Simmer gently until reduced to about half its original volume, then stir in the double cream. Cook for a further 2 minutes.

Serve the mushroom parcels with the sauce poured round them and garnished with chopped chives or parsley.

*Germain Schwab, Winteringham Fields, South Humberside*

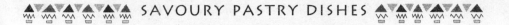 

# VEGETABLE SAMOSAS

*Makes about 15*

1 medium potato, cut into small cubes
50 g (2 oz) frozen mixed vegetables
$\frac{1}{2}$ teaspoon mild curry paste
2 tablespoons full-fat soft cheese
salt and freshly ground black pepper
about 5 large sheets of filo pastry
vegetable oil for brushing
poppy seeds for sprinkling

Preheat the oven to 190°C (375°F, Gas Mark 5). Cook the potato in boiling salted water for about 10 minutes, until tender. Add the frozen vegetables and cook for 2 minutes longer, then drain. Transfer the vegetables to a bowl, add the curry paste, cheese and a little salt and pepper and mix well. Leave to cool.

Lay the filo sheets one on top of the other on a work surface and cut lengthways into strips about 8 cm (3 inch) wide. Take one strip and put a teaspoon of the filling at one end. Fold the top of the pastry diagonally across the filling so that it makes a triangle, then keep folding along the length of the pastry. Repeat with the remaining pastry and filling.

Put the samosas on a baking sheet, brush with a little oil and sprinkle with poppy seeds. Bake in the oven for 15–20 minutes or until golden brown. Serve warm or cold.

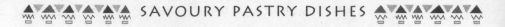 

# LEEK AND ALMOND FILO FLAN

*Serves 6*

125 g (4 oz) butter or 125 ml (4 fl oz) sunflower oil
2 garlic cloves, crushed
750 g (1 1/2 lb) leeks, white and light green parts only, shredded
50 g (2 oz) ground almonds
a little vegetable stock (optional)
salt and freshly ground black pepper
250 g (8 oz) filo pastry
1–2 tablespoons sesame seeds

*For the leek and watercress sauce*
1 oz butter
150 g (5 oz) leeks, white and light green parts only, shredded
450 ml (3/4 pint) vegetable stock
bunch of watercress

Preheat the oven to 190°C (375°F, Gas Mark 5). Melt half the butter or sunflower oil in a pan, add the garlic and cook gently until softened. Add the leeks, cover and cook gently for about 10 minutes, until the leeks are soft and the juices have been released. Stir in the ground almonds. If the mixture is too dry add a little vegetable stock. Season well, then turn into a shallow dish to cool.

Grease a 23 cm (9 inch) flan tin. If using butter, melt the remaining butter over a low heat. Brush the filo sheets with melted butter or sunflower oil and layer them in the flan tin, draping the excess over the sides. Place the leek and almond filling in the centre, smooth the top and draw up the filo to give a crumpled effect on top. Brush with more melted butter or sunflower oil and sprinkle the sesame seeds over. Bake for 25 minutes. Just before it is cooked carefully remove the flan ring and return the flan to the oven for the last 5 minutes.

To make the sauce, melt the butter in a pan, add the leeks and mix well, then cover and cook gently for 5 minutes. Add the vegetable stock, bring to the boil, then reduce the heat and simmer for 10 minutes. Finely chop the watercress, removing any large stalks. Reserve a few good leaves. Add the chopped watercress to the leek mixture and cook for a further 2–3 minutes – no longer or it will lose its colour. Cool slightly then purée in a food processor or liquidizer until smooth. Reheat gently, stir in the reserved watercress leaves and season to taste.

Serve the flan with the leek and watercress sauce. It is also good served with tomato or tomato and watercress sauce.

*Don Hacker, Birmingham College of Food*

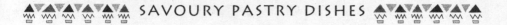 

# LEEK, CHEESE AND MUSHROOM STRUDEL

*Serves 4–6*

*This recipe is a bit different for vegetarians and exciting to make.*

1 red pepper
250 g (8 oz) leeks, finely sliced
125 g (4 oz) mushrooms, sliced
1 tablespoon olive oil
200 g (7oz) cooked brown rice
125 g (4 oz) Cheddar cheese, grated
$^1/_2$ tsp dried thyme
salt and freshly ground black pepper
250 g (8 oz) filo pastry
50 g (2 oz) butter, melted
1 tablespoon sesame seeds

Place the red pepper under a very hot grill and cook until blackened and blistered on all sides. Leave until cool enough to handle, then peel off the skin, deseed the pepper and cut it into strips.

Preheat the oven to 200°C (400°F, Gas Mark 6). Put the leeks, mushrooms and olive oil in a bowl, cover and microwave on high for 5 minutes. Mix with the rice, cheese and thyme, then season lightly with salt and pepper.

Brush the sheets of filo pastry with the melted butter and layer them to form a 40 cm (16 inch) square, overlapping the sheets and trimming them if necessary. Place the filling on top, leaving a 2 cm ($^3/_4$ inch) border all round. Lay strips of red pepper on top of the filling, then fold in the sides of the pastry and roll up. Place on a greased baking tray with the join underneath. Brush with melted butter and sprinkle with the sesame seeds. Bake in the oven for 25–30 minutes, until golden brown. Serve with a tomato or celery sauce, if liked.

*Sarah Moreton (aged 10), Milnthorpe, Cumbria*

# VEGETARIAN PLAIT

*Serves 4*

*This is my favourite vegetarian meal because it's cheap, tasty and looks nice. I recently made it for a fund-raising meal for my friends and they all really enjoyed it.*

1 tablespoon sunflower oil
1 medium onion, chopped
2 leeks, chopped
175 g (6 oz) mushrooms, chopped
1 large tomato, chopped
425 g (15 oz) can of kidney beans, drained
1 tablespoon chopped fresh basil
salt and freshly ground black pepper
250 g (8 oz) puff pastry
1 egg, beaten

Preheat the oven to 200°C (400°F, Gas Mark 6). Heat the oil in a pan and fry the onion, leeks and mushrooms until soft. Add the tomato and the kidney beans and cook gently for a few minutes just to heat through. Stir in the basil and season to taste with salt and pepper.

Roll out the puff pastry quite thinly on a lightly floured work surface and arrange the vegetable mixture in a line down the middle. Slash the edges of the pastry in diagonal lines about 2.5 cm (1 inch) apart, going almost up to the filling. Then, starting at the top, fold the pastry sections over each other to cover the filling, so that you get a plaited effect. Brush with the beaten egg and bake for 30–40 minutes, until golden brown. Cool slightly, then cut into slices to serve.

*Eleanor Standen, Loughborough, Leicestershire*

# VEGETABLE PIE

*Serves 6*

*This is a good everyday pie for family meals. The vegetables used can be adapted to suit children's likes and dislikes.*

4 tablespoons olive oil
1 large onion, chopped
2 large carrots, diced
2 medium courgettes, diced
250 g (8 oz) broccoli, divided into small florets
250 g (8 oz) mushrooms, quartered
2 tablespoons plain flour
2 tablespoons tomato purée
2 tablespoons soy sauce
1 dessertspoon vegetarian Worcestershire sauce
300 ml ($1/_2$ pint) water
salt and freshly ground black pepper

*For the pastry*
250 g (8 oz) plain flour
125 g (4 oz) sunflower margarine
a pinch of salt

To make the pastry, put the flour, margarine and salt in a food processor and process with enough water to give a pliable dough. Alternatively, make the pastry in the conventional way, rubbing the margarine into the flour and salt and stirring in the water. Wrap in cling film and put in the fridge while you make the filling. Preheat the oven to 200°C (400°F, Gas Mark 6).

Heat the oil in a large saucepan, add the onion and cook for 5 minutes, until starting to soften. Add the carrots and cook for another 5 minutes, stirring occasionally to prevent browning. Stir in the courgettes, broccoli and mushrooms, then cover and cook for 5 minutes. Add the flour, mix well, then add the tomato purée, soy sauce and Worcestershire sauce. Stir in the water and bring slowly to the boil, stirring constantly. Reduce the heat and continue to stir until the sauce thickens. Add more water if necessary to give a generous amount of thickened sauce. Cook over a gentle heat for another 5 minutes, then transfer the mixture to an oval pie dish and leave to cool.

Roll out the pastry and use to cover the vegetable mixture. Decorate with pastry trimmings and make steam holes. Bake in the oven for 35–40 minutes, until the pastry is golden brown. Serve with creamed potatoes and peas.

*Jenny Mathers, Oxfam volunteer, Riding Mill, Northumberland*

# POTATO CREAM PIE

250 g (8 oz) flaky pastry or puff pastry
3 large potatoes (about 625 g/ 1 1/4 lb), thinly sliced
1 small onion, finely chopped
1 tablespoon chopped fresh parsley
1 tablespoon chopped fresh chives
15 g (1/2 oz) butter
salt and freshly ground black pepper
125–150 ml (4–5 fl oz) single cream

Preheat the oven to 200°C (400°F, Gas Mark 6). Roll out half the pastry thinly and use to line a 23 cm (9 inch) pie plate. Arrange the sliced potatoes on the pastry and sprinkle over the onion and herbs, then dot with the butter and season. Roll out the remaining pastry thinly and use to cover the pie, pressing the edges together well to seal. Bake in the oven for 30 minutes, then remove from the oven and make a slit in the centre. Pour in the cream and return the pie to the oven for about 15 minutes. Test with a knife; if the potatoes are not tender, cover the pie with foil, reduce the heat to 180°C (350°F, Gas Mark 4) and bake for a further 10–15 minutes. Serve hot.

*Laura Evans, Corwen, Clwyd*

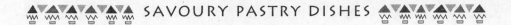

# BOREK

*Makes about 30*

*Middle Eastern cooking is colourful, rich and scented with spices. It's a very hospitable part of the world and food plays a big part in making visitors welcome. A typical Middle Eastern meal begins with a tableful of starters called* mezze. *As well as these little pies, you might be offered olives, pickles, nuts, salads and dips such as hummus (see page 17).*

375 g (12 oz) feta cheese
a large bunch of mint, stalks removed, leaves chopped
freshly ground black pepper
freshly grated nutmeg
250 g (8 oz) filo pastry
4 tablespoons olive oil

Preheat the oven to 180°C (350°F, Gas Mark 4). Crumble the feta cheese into a bowl, add the chopped mint, season with pepper and nutmeg and mash with a fork until creamy.

Cut the filo pastry into strips about 8 cm (3 inch) wide. Brush with the olive oil and put a teaspoonful of the feta mixture in the top corner of each one. Fold the pastry over the filling and continue folding to the end of the pastry to form a triangle. Brush with more oil and bake on a greased baking tray for 25 minutes, or until golden.

# LUNCHBOX PIZZA

*Serves 4*

*This is tasty and nutritious, a good addition to children's lunchboxes.*

1 tablespoon olive or vegetable oil
1 large onion, chopped
1 red pepper, finely chopped
1 green pepper, finely chopped
65 g (2$^1/_2$ oz) tomato purée
250 g (8 oz) can of tomatoes
2 teaspoons chopped fresh basil or 1 teaspoon dried basil
freshly ground black pepper
4 tomatoes, sliced (optional)
50 g (2 oz) Cheddar cheese, grated
1 tablespoon freshly grated Parmesan cheese

*For the base*
250 g (8 oz) plain wholemeal flour
1 teaspoon baking powder
a small pinch of salt
50 g (2 oz) polyunsaturated margarine
1 egg, beaten
4 tablespoons skimmed milk

Preheat the oven to 200°C (400°F, Gas Mark 6). Heat the oil in a saucepan, add the onion and peppers and cook gently for 5 minutes. Stir in the tomato purée, canned tomatoes and basil and season with black pepper. Cook for about 10 minutes, until thickened, then remove from the heat and leave to cool.

Grease a 30 x 20 cm (12 x 8 inch) baking tray. Mix the flour, baking powder and salt together in a bowl and rub in the margarine. Mix to a soft dough with the egg and milk, then turn out on to a floured surface and knead lightly until smooth.

Roll out the dough to a rectangle to fit the baking tray and spread the tomato sauce over it. Arrange the fresh tomatoes on top, if using, and sprinkle over the Cheddar and Parmesan cheese. Bake in the oven for 25–30 minutes, until the base is cooked through and the cheese is browned. Serve cut into slices. You can leave the pizza to cool and then wrap it in foil, ready to pack into lunchboxes for school.

*Martha Reid, Dublin*

# QUICK PIZZA

*Serves 4*

*Pizza is always fun to make and fun to eat. The great thing is that you can put on your favourite toppings. The crust is a bit simpler in this recipe than for most pizzas, since you don't have to knead it.*

3 tablespoons olive oil
1 onion, chopped
1 garlic clove, crushed
500 g (1 lb) tomatoes, peeled and chopped
1–2 tablespoons tomato purée (optional)
1 tablespoon chopped fresh basil
salt and freshly ground black pepper
toppings of your choice – thinly sliced peppers or mushrooms, sweetcorn,
sliced courgettes, fresh or sun-dried tomatoes, etc.
125 g (4 oz) mozzarella cheese, grated

*For the base*
250 g (8 oz) self-raising flour
$\frac{1}{2}$ teaspoon salt
1 teaspoon dried basil and oregano
2 tablespoons olive oil
about 125 ml (4 fl oz) water

To make the base, sift the flour and salt into a bowl, stir in the dried herbs and make a well in the centre. Pour in the oil and enough water to make a dough that is soft but not sticky. Set aside.

To make the topping, heat 1 tablespoon of the olive oil in a pan and fry the onion and garlic until soft. Add the tomatoes, tomato purée, if using, basil and salt and pepper to taste. Simmer for 20–25 minutes until reduced to a fairly thick consistency.

Roll the dough out on a lightly floured surface to a 25 cm (10 inch) circle. Heat 1 tablespoon of the remaining oil in a 25 cm (10 inch) frying pan and fry the pizza base on a low heat for 5 minutes. Turn and cook the other side in the remaining oil. While the second side is cooking, spread the tomato sauce on top of the pizza base and then add your favourite toppings.

When the second side is cooked, sprinkle the mozzarella cheese over the top and place the pizza under a hot grill for a few minutes until the cheese bubbles.

*Roberta Jordan, St Peter Port, Guernsey*

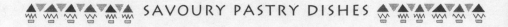 

# CALZONE

*Makes 6*

*Calzone is essentially a pizza that has been folded over like a turnover, then baked.*

625 g (1¼ lb) packet of white bread mix
flour for dusting
2 tablespoons freshly grated Parmesan cheese
1 egg, beaten
375 g (12 oz) potatoes, cooked and mashed
250 g (8 oz) Cheddar cheese, grated
(or use a mixture of Cheddar and mozzarella)
jar of pizza topping or tomato purée for spreading
1 teaspoon dried mixed Italian herbs

Preheat the oven to 220°C (425°F, Gas Mark 7). Make up the dough according to the instructions on the packet. Sprinkle a work surface with a little flour and the Parmesan cheese, then roll out the dough and cut out six 15 cm (6 inch) circles. Brush the edge of each one with beaten egg.

Gently mix together the potatoes and grated cheese. Spread a little tomato topping on each round and sprinkle with the herbs. Spoon the potato mixture on to one half of each round, fold over the dough and press the edges together well to seal.

Place the calzone on a lightly greased baking tray and prick each one once or twice with a fork. Brush with beaten egg and bake in the oven for about 15–20 minutes, until golden brown.

*Valerie Barrett*

# PASTA

# REALLY GOOD QUICK MACARONI CHEESE

*Serves 4*

*Macaroni cheese is always popular with children but many recipes, I find, are far too stodgy. This one is good and light.*

125 g (4 oz) macaroni
50 g (2 oz) butter or margarine
40 g (1$^1/_2$ oz) plain flour
600 ml (1 pint) milk
175 g (6 oz) Cheddar cheese, grated
$^1/_2$ teaspoon mustard powder
salt and freshly ground black pepper
50 g (2 oz) soft fresh breadcrumbs

Preheat the oven to 200°C (400°F, Gas Mark 6). Cook the macaroni in plenty of boiling water until just tender, then drain. Meanwhile, make a sauce: melt the butter or margarine in a saucepan and then stir in the flour. When it froths at the edges add a third of the milk and cook, stirring, for a few seconds until it thickens. Add another third and repeat the process until all the milk has been added. You will end up with a thin sauce, but don't worry; the whole thing thickens up once the macaroni has been added. Let it simmer for a few minutes, then remove from the heat and add two-thirds of the cheese plus the mustard, macaroni and salt and pepper to taste. Pour the mixture into an ovenproof dish, top with the crumbs and the rest of the cheese and bake for 30–40 minutes, until crisp and golden brown.

*Rose Elliot*

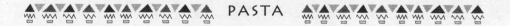 

# SPAGHETTI WITH LENTIL SAUCE

*Serves 2–3*

1 tablespoon olive oil
1 onion, chopped
1–2 garlic cloves, crushed
250 g (8 oz) can of tomatoes
425 g (14 oz) can of green lentils, drained
1 tablespoon tomato purée or sun-dried tomato purée
250 g (8 oz) spaghetti
15 g ($^1/_2$ oz) butter
salt and freshly ground black pepper
freshly grated Parmesan cheese and/or torn basil leaves or
chopped fresh parsley, to serve

Heat the oil in a pan, add the onion, then cover and cook gently for 10 minutes. Add the garlic and stir for a moment, then add the tomatoes, chopping them up with a spoon. Stir in the lentils and tomato purée, then simmer, uncovered, for 10–15 minutes until the liquid has reduced a little. Meanwhile, cook the spaghetti in a large pan of boiling salted water for about 8 minutes, until just tender, then drain it and return to the pan. Stir in the butter and salt and pepper to taste. Season the sauce with salt and pepper and serve with the spaghetti, either mixed in or spooned on top, with some grated Parmesan and/or basil or parsley.

*Rose Elliot*

# EASY-PEASY PASTA

*Serves 2*

*One of my daughter Claire's favourites. You could vary this recipe by using frozen sweetcorn instead of peas and another type of smooth, creamy cheese instead of the low-fat Boursin.*

200 g (7 oz) pasta shapes, such as fusilli, farfalle, penne or rigatoni
125 g (4 oz) frozen peas, preferably petit pois
125 g (4 oz) low-fat Boursin cheese
salt and freshly ground black pepper

Bring a large pan of water to the boil, then add the pasta. Stir, then boil until just tender, about 7–10 minutes. Just before the pasta is done, add the peas. Drain the pasta and the peas into a colander, then return them to the pan and add the Boursin and some salt and pepper to taste. Mix gently until everything is combined, then serve.

*Rose Elliot*

In Pabban village, south-east Pakistan, there are hundreds of acres of mango orchards. But when the area flooded in 1992 most of the orchards were destroyed. The Fruit Farm Development Organization, funded by Oxfam, has helped the villagers find ways of bringing life back to the orchards: by planting eucalyptus trees which soak up water; by using compost; by making drainage canals.

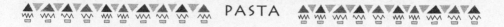 

# LEEK AND MUSHROOM CANNELLONI

*Serves 2 adults and 1 child*

*Some may think this recipe unsuitable for children because of the strong taste of leeks and onions, but my 16-month-old son Harri loves it. However, he seems to love every-thing I give him so I can hardly claim he has a discerning palette. You can use fresh lasagne to make your own cannelloni if you prefer – simply roll them up like sausage rolls.*

1 large leek
1 medium onion
olive oil for frying
125 g (4 oz) mushrooms, very finely chopped
1 smoked cheese roll, sliced, or
125–175 g (4–6 oz) well-flavoured cheese, grated
1 small onion, finely chopped
400 g (13 oz) can of tomatoes
1 vegetable stock cube
300 ml (¹/₂ pint) hot water
a dash of vegetarian Worcestershire sauce
15 no-need-to-precook cannelloni tubes

Preheat the oven to 190°C (375°F, Gas Mark 5) or according to the instructions on the cannelloni packet. Using a blender or food processor, chop the leek and medium onion into very small pieces. Heat some olive oil in a pan and fry them until softened. Add the mushrooms, then break the cheese into the pan and cook, stirring, until the vegetables are golden. Once the cheese has melted into the mixture, remove from the heat and leave to cool.

Meanwhile, in a separate pan fry the small onion in a little oil until brown. Stir in the tomatoes. Mix the stock cube with the hot water and add to the onion and tomatoes with the Worcestershire sauce. Cook the mixture until reduced by half.

Fill the cannelloni with the leek and cheese mixture and place them in a greased ovenproof dish. Pour over the tomato sauce and bake for 25–30 minutes. Serve with ciabatta bread.

*Sharanne Basham-Pyke, Newport, Gwent*

# HOME-MADE TAGLIATELLE
# WITH VEGETABLE SAUCE

*Serves 4*

2 eggs
250 g (8 oz) plain or wholemeal flour
a pinch of sea salt

*For the sauce*
olive oil for frying
2 small onions, chopped
2 garlic cloves, crushed
3 tomatoes, chopped
1 green pepper, chopped
1 carrot, finely chopped
a selection of vegetables, such as broccoli,
aubergine and courgette, chopped
1 chilli, deseeded and finely chopped (optional)
chopped fresh herbs, such as thyme, oregano,
rosemary, basil, parsley or chives, to taste
salt and freshly ground black pepper

Put the eggs, flour and salt into a food processor and process until they form a ball. Place the dough on a floured work surface, flatten it slightly and, if it is sticky, knead in a little extra flour by hand. Using a pasta machine, guide the ball through the 2 rollers and turn the handle. Repeat this operation until the pasta gets thinner and thinner, adjusting the rollers until you have reached position 6. As the pasta gets longer, cut it into pieces to make it easier to handle. Put it through the cutters to make tagliatelle, then drape it over the back of a kitchen chair or lay it on a clean tea towel to dry.

Meanwhile make the sauce. Heat some olive oil in a frying pan, add the onions and garlic and cook for one minute, then stir in all the remaining vegetables and herbs. Season and cook gently until the vegetables are just tender.

To cook the pasta, bring a large pan of water to the boil and add 1 tablespoon of olive oil. Carefully add the tagliatelle to the pan. It should only take 30 seconds to cook and should still be *al dente*. Drain and serve immediately, with the sauce poured over.

*Mieke Stephenson, Hale Barns, Cheshire*

# SPEEDY PASTA

*Serves 3*

1 onion, chopped
125 g (4 oz) mushrooms, chopped
vegetable oil for frying
425 g (15 oz) can of mushroom or celery cream soup
$^1/_2$ × 425 g (15 oz can) of kidney beans, drained
$^1/_2$ × 325 g (11 oz) can of sweetcorn, drained
175 g (6 oz) egg and spinach tagliatelle
50 g (2 oz) Parmesan cheese, freshly grated

Fry the onion and mushrooms in a little oil until tender. In a separate pan, heat the soup and add the beans and sweetcorn. Stir in the onion and mushrooms. Cook the pasta in plenty of boiling water for 8 minutes, until just tender, then drain. Transfer to a serving dish, pour over the sauce and sprinkle with the cheese.

*Irene Hopgood, South Croydon, Surrey*

# PASTA BOWS WITH THREE CHEESES

*Serves 2–3*

250 g (8 oz) pasta bows
25 g (1 oz) butter
1 tablespoon plain flour
300 ml ($^1/_2$ pint) milk
50 g (2 oz) Gruyère cheese, grated
50 g (2 oz) Gorgonzola cheese, grated
50 g (2 oz) mozzarella cheese, grated

Cook the pasta bows in plenty of lightly salted boiling water for about 8–10 minutes, or until just tender but not too soft. Meanwhile, heat the butter in a saucepan, add the flour and cook for 1 minute. Gradually add the milk, stirring all the time, then bring to the boil and cook until the sauce is smooth and thickened, about 5 minutes. Remove from the heat and stir in all the cheese. Drain the pasta, pour the cheese sauce over and mix thoroughly.

*Annabel Karmel*

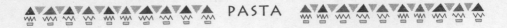 

# MRS B'S SPECIAL

*Serves 4*

*This is great fun to eat and very tasty. Mrs B was a wonderful old lady who used to make it for me when I was a child.*

2 tablespoons olive oil
1 large onion, chopped
1 large red pepper, chopped
2 garlic cloves, chopped
400 g (13 oz) can of tomatoes
$\frac{1}{2}$ teaspoon cayenne pepper
salt and freshly ground black pepper
375 g (12 oz) spaghetti
125 g (4 oz) Cheddar cheese, grated

Heat half the oil in a frying pan, add the onion, red pepper and garlic and cook until softened. Add the tomatoes and cayenne pepper, cover and cook gently for 10–15 minutes, then season with salt and pepper. Meanwhile, bring to the boil a large pan of water, add the remaining oil, then add the spaghetti and cook until just tender. Drain and return the spaghetti to the pan, then add the sauce. Sprinkle on the grated cheese and serve immediately.

*Chris Griffiths, Oxfam vehicles unit*

# HOME-MADE TOMATO SAUCE FOR PASTA

*Makes 900 ml (1¹/₂ pints)*

*Pasta and tomato sauce is an all-time favourite with most children. I always make more than I need and store some in plastic containers in the freezer. You could add a chopped pepper, carrot or courgette and sauté these together with the onion. For a very smooth sauce, put it through a sieve to get rid of the tomato pips. Another idea is to make a creamy sauce by stirring in some Philadelphia cheese or mascarpone.*

*I often add skinned fresh tomatoes to bump up the vitamin content a little and then season it with Italian seasoning. This is an excellent way of getting your children to eat their vegetables!*

1 onion, chopped
1 garlic clove, crushed
1 tablespoon olive oil
2 tablespoons tomato purée
2 × 400 g (13 oz) cans of chopped tomatoes
¹/₂ teaspoon sugar
1 tablespoon chopped fresh parsley
a handful of fresh basil, chopped, or 1 teaspoon dried basil or oregano
salt and freshly ground black pepper

Saute the onion and garlic in the oil until softened. Add the tomato purée and cook for 2 minutes. Stir in the chopped tomatoes, sugar and herbs, then simmer, uncovered, until the sauce thickens, about 15 minutes. Season to taste with salt and pepper. Serve with the pasta of your choice.

*Annabel Karmel*

# VEGETARIAN LASAGNE

*Serves 2–3*

*This is my favourite recipe for lasagne. It's absolutely delicious and children love it. I prefer to use traditional lasagne that has to be cooked in water first because it has a much nicer texture than the type that needs no pre-cooking. The added bonus is that once it's been cooked, you can cut it down to fit the size of your dish.*

6 lasagne sheets, dried or fresh
1 teaspoon vegetable oil
250 g (8 oz) frozen spinach or 500 g (1 lb) fresh spinach
15 g ($^1/_2$ oz) butter
175 g (6 oz) ricotta or cottage cheese
1 egg, lightly beaten
2 tablespoons double cream
25 g (1 oz) Parmesan or Gruyère cheese, freshly grated,
plus 1 tablespoon for the topping
600 ml (1 pint) Home-Made Tomato Sauce (see page 71)
125 g (4 oz) mozzarella cheese, grated

Preheat the oven to 180°C (350°F, Gas Mark 4). Cook the lasagne in plenty of lightly salted boiling water until just tender, adding the oil to prevent the sheets sticking together. Drain, then rinse under cold running water and separate the sheets. I hang them over the side of a colander.

Cook the spinach and drain thoroughly, squeezing out as much water as possible, then fry it briefly in the butter. Mix thoroughly with the ricotta or cottage cheese, egg, cream and Parmesan or Gruyère.

To assemble the lasagne, spread a quarter of the tomato sauce over the base of a 15 cm (6 inch) square ovenproof dish or small oval gratin dish and lay 2 sheets of lasagne on top. Cover with half the spinach mixture, a third of the mozzarella and a quarter of the tomato sauce. Again lay 2 sheets of lasagne on top and repeat the layers. Lay two more sheets of lasagne on top and cover with the remaining tomato sauce. Sprinkle over the rest of the mozzarella and the extra Parmesan or Gruyère. Bake in the oven for about 30–35 minutes, until golden brown.

*Annabel Karmel*

# TOFU AND PEANUT BUTTER STIR-FRY WITH NOODLES

*Serves 2*

*Tofu is high in protein and low in fat. Although tasteless on its own, it blends well with other flavours. This delicious mix of crunchy vegetables, tofu and noodles was specially concocted for my daughter, Lara, whose favourite foods are peanut butter and pasta.*

50 g (2 oz) thin egg noodles
2 tablespoons soy sauce
2 tablespoons smooth peanut butter
1 teaspoon brown sugar
4 tablespoons sesame or sunflower oil
275 g (9 oz) firm tofu, cut into 1 cm ($^1/_2$ inch) cubes and rolled in flour
3 spring onions, finely sliced
75 g (3 oz) Chinese cabbage, shredded
4 baby sweetcorn
150 g (5 oz) beansprouts

Cook the noodles according to the instructions on the packet and set aside. Mix together the soy sauce, peanut butter and sugar.

In a wok or large frying pan, heat 3 tablespoons of the oil and fry the tofu until golden brown on all sides. Remove from the pan and set aside. Heat the remaining oil in the pan and sauté the spring onions for 1 minute. Add the cabbage, baby corn and beansprouts and continue to cook for a couple of minutes. Return the tofu to the pan with the noodles and the peanut sauce. Mix thoroughly and cook gently for a couple of minutes to heat through.

*Annabel Karmel*

# ANIMAL PASTA SALAD WITH MULTI-COLOURED VEGETABLES

*Serves 2*

*I make this salad with multi-coloured animal-shaped pasta. It looks very attractive and colourful on a plate and children love picking out all the different ingredients. It can be served warm or cold and you can vary the vegetables according to what your child likes the best.*

125 g (4 oz) multi-coloured novelty-shaped pasta
50 g (2 oz) cauliflower, cut into small florets
50 g (2 oz) broccoli, cut into small florets
50 g (2 oz) French beans
1 medium courgette, cut into strips
75 g (3 oz) frozen sweetcorn
15 g ($^1/_2$ oz) butter
$^1/_4$ red pepper, cut into strips
65 g ($2^1/_2$ oz) button mushrooms, sliced

*For the dressing*
2 tablespoons red wine vinegar or cider vinegar
salt and freshly ground black pepper
2 tablespoons apple juice
3 tablespoons walnut oil or olive oil
$1^1/_2$ tablespoons chopped fresh chives or finely sliced spring onion

Cook the pasta in plenty of boiling salted water until just tender, then drain. Meanwhile, steam the cauliflower, broccoli and French beans for 3 minutes, then add the courgette strips and sweetcorn and cook for 3 minutes longer.

Heat the butter in a pan and sauté the red pepper and mushrooms for 3–4 minutes, until tender. In a salad bowl, mix together all the cooked vegetables and the pasta.

To make the dressing, whisk together the vinegar and salt and pepper, then whisk in the apple juice and oil a little at a time. Add the chives or spring onion and pour the dressing over the salad.

*Annabel Karmel*

# PASTA WITH AUBERGINE SAUCE

*Serves 4*

*This recipe unites a number of my favourite things: garlic, chilli, aubergine, tomatoes and – probably the most frequently consumed food in our household – pasta. There are hundreds of aubergine and pasta recipes from all over Italy (where my family and I often spend holidays) and this one seems to borrow heavily from all of them! The most interesting twist here is that the aubergine is boiled rather than fried, which results in a more delicate sauce. I owe this innovation to Carla Camporesi and her wonderful cookbook* Un boccone insieme.

1 large aubergine, cut into cubes
2–4 tablespoons good-quality olive oil
2 garlic cloves, chopped
2 dried red chillies, or to taste
400 g (13 oz) can of chopped tomatoes or passata
salt and freshly ground black pepper
375 g (12 oz) pasta of your choice
freshly grated Parmesan cheese, to serve

Cook the aubergine in boiling salted water until just tender, then drain and set aside. Pour some olive oil into a saucepan and heat over a moderate flame. Add the garlic and fry gently for 2–3 minutes, then crumble in the chillies. Continue to fry until the garlic softens, but don't let it brown. Add the tomatoes, reduce the heat and cook, stirring occasionally, for about 15 minutes. Add the cooked aubergine and season with salt and pepper.

Cook the pasta in a large pan of boiling salted water until *ul dente*. Drain and add to the sauce, mixing them together well. Tip into a heated serving dish and serve with Parmesan cheese.

*Loyd Grossman*

# VEGETARIAN SPAGHETTI

*Serves 4*

1 aubergine, cut into 1 cm ($^1/_2$ inch) chunks
salt and freshly ground black pepper
2 tablespoons olive oil
1 onion, chopped
1 garlic clove, crushed
1 courgette, cut into chunks
1 red pepper, diced
1 yellow pepper, diced
2 carrots, finely diced
400 g (13 oz) can of chopped tomatoes
375 g (12 oz) spaghetti
about 6 basil leaves, shredded
freshly grated Parmesan cheese, to serve

Sprinkle $^1/_2$ teaspoon of salt over the aubergine and leave for 15 minutes. Rinse with cold water and pat dry on kitchen paper.

Heat the olive oil in a frying pan and add the aubergine and all the other vegetables except the tomatoes. Fry gently for about 5 minutes, stirring occasionally. Add the tomatoes, season to taste and simmer for 10 minutes, until the vegetables are just tender but not overcooked.

Meanwhile, cook the spaghetti in a large pan of boiling salted water until just tender, then drain. Add the basil to the vegetable sauce and mix well with the spaghetti. Serve topped with Parmesan cheese and accompanied by crusty bread.

*Toby Anstis*

# RICE & GRAINS

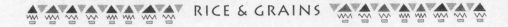 

# POLENTA ANIMALS WITH PARSLEY SAUCE

*Serves 4*

*Polenta can be left to set on a plate, then cut into shapes and fried or grilled. It makes a kind of vegetarian 'fish finger' replacement, which is popular with children. Use cutters to cut it into animal shapes, if you like. Here it is served with a bright green parsley sauce. Healthy Home-made Oven Chips (see page 113) also go well with it.*

600 ml (1 pint) water
2 teaspoons salt
175 g (6 oz) fine polenta – instant if you can get it
125 g (4 oz) Cheddar cheese, grated
oil for shallow-frying
lemon wedges, to serve

*For the parsley sauce*
25 g (1 oz) butter or margarine
25 g (1 oz) plain flour
450 ml ($^3/_4$ pint) milk
4 tablespoons chopped fresh parsley
salt and freshly ground black pepper

Put the water into a pan with the salt and bring to the boil. Sprinkle the polenta on top, stirring; continue to stir over the heat until the mixture is smooth, then leave it over a gentle heat until thick. This will take about 4 minutes with instant polenta, 40–60 minutes with normal polenta – be guided by the instructions on the packet. Remove the polenta from the heat and stir in the cheese. Press the mixture out on to a plate or baking tray in a layer about 5 mm ($^1/_4$ inch) thick and leave it to cool and firm up.

Meanwhile, make the sauce. Melt the butter or margarine in a medium pan, then stir in the flour. When it froths at the edges add the milk, stirring well. Stir until it thickens, then leave it over a very gentle heat for 7–10 minutes to cook the flour. Remove from the heat, add the parsley and season to taste.

Cut the polenta into shapes and shallow-fry them in hot oil until lightly browned – they won't get very brown but they will become crisp. Turn them over and cook the second side, then drain them on kitchen paper. Reheat the sauce and serve the polenta shapes with the parsley sauce and wedges of lemon.

*Rose Elliot*

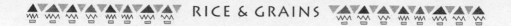 

# CELERY RICE

*Serves 4*

*I'm not sure why this is popular with children but, in my experience, it is. It's good served with some crisp lettuce leaves which can be used as 'scoops' for eating it.*

2 tablespoons olive oil
1 large onion, chopped
4–6 celery sticks, sliced
1 red pepper, chopped
2 garlic cloves, crushed
2 tomatoes, skinned and chopped
250 g (8 oz) brown rice
600 ml (1 pint) water
2 tablespoons chopped fresh parsley
salt and freshly ground black pepper

Heat the oil in a heavy-based saucepan, then add the onion and celery; cover and cook gently for 10 minutes, until the vegetables are beginning to soften. Stir in the red pepper, garlic, tomatoes and rice, then add the water. Bring to the boil, cover and leave to cook over a very low heat for 40–45 minutes, until all the liquid has been absorbed and the rice is tender. Add the parsley and salt and pepper to taste, stirring them in gently with a fork, then serve.

*Rose Elliot*

In 2800 BC China named five sacred cops – rice,
soya beans, wheat, maize and barley.

# VEGETABLE COUSCOUS

*Serves 6*

*For a more elaborate dish, stir a few toasted flaked almonds and a handful of chopped fresh coriander into the cooked couscous grains.*

125 g (4 oz) chick peas, soaked overnight
250 g (8 oz) couscous
450 ml ($^3/_4$ pint) water
1 tablespoon vegetable oil
2 onions, chopped
1 garlic clove, crushed
1 teaspoon ground cumin
1 teaspoon ground coriander
$^1/_4$ teaspoon chilli powder
2 leeks, sliced
2 carrots, sliced
600 ml (1 pint) vegetable stock
3 courgettes, sliced
1 large tomato, coarsely chopped
50 g (2 oz) raisins
50 g (2 oz) no-need-to-soak dried apricots

Drain the chick peas, put them in a saucepan and cover with cold water. Bring to the boil and boil rapidly for 10–15 minutes. Reduce the heat and simmer for 40–50 minutes or until tender, then drain.

Meanwhile, put the couscous in a bowl and pour over the water. Leave to soak for 10–15 minutes or until the water has been absorbed.

Heat the oil in a large saucepan, add the onions and cook for 5 minutes. Add the garlic and spices and cook, stirring, for 1 minute. Add the leeks, carrots and stock and bring to the boil.

Line a large sieve with muslin or a clean J-cloth and place it over the vegetable stew. Put the couscous in the sieve, cover the whole pan with foil to enclose the steam and simmer the stew for 20 minutes. Add the chick peas, courgettes, tomato, raisins and apricots to the stew, replace the sieve and fluff up the couscous with a fork. Cover and simmer for 10 minutes, then serve the stew with the couscous.

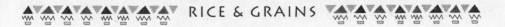 

# GNOCCHI

*Serves 6*

*The soft, unchallenging texture of these little Italian 'dumplings' makes them suitable for very young children. Use a variety of canned tomatoes without extra juice or they will make the finished dish too wet.*

175 g (6 oz) semolina
900 ml (1½ pints) milk
salt and freshly ground black pepper
1 egg
125 g (4 oz) mature Cheddar cheese, grated
400 g (13 oz) can of chopped tomatoes
25 g (1 oz) butter
freshly grated Parmesan cheese or
extra grated Cheddar cheese, for sprinkling

Put the semolina and milk in a non-stick pan and bring to the boil, stirring all the time. Cook over a high heat for about 3 minutes or until very thick. Remove from the heat and season with salt and pepper. Add the egg and cheese, mix thoroughly and leave to cool.

Pour the tomatoes into a shallow heatproof dish, spreading them out into a thin layer. Season with a little salt and pepper.

Shape the gnocchi mixture into small balls and arrange in a single layer on top of the tomatoes. Dot with butter and sprinkle generously with cheese. Cook under a hot grill for 5–10 minutes or until the gnocchi are cooked through and the cheese has melted and is golden brown and bubbling.

In 1970, after decades of modernization, Japanese
rice farming was still very labour intensive. It took
1,729 hours of labour each year to produce every
hectare of rice whereas American wheat farmers used
just seven hours per hectare.

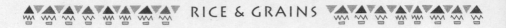

# MOROCCAN RICE

*Serves 4*

2 tablespoons oil
1 onion, chopped
1 garlic clove, finely chopped
2 teaspoons finely grated fresh ginger root
1 teaspoon ground cumin
1 teaspoon ground coriander
$1/_2$ teaspoon ground turmeric
1 teaspoon paprika
250 g (8 oz) long grain rice
450 ml ($3/_4$ pint) vegetable stock
400 g (13 oz) can of chopped tomatoes
2 courgettes, chopped
50 g (2 oz) fresh or frozen peas
50 g (2 oz) sweetcorn
50 g (2 oz) raisins
50 g (2 oz) no-need-to-soak dried apricots, chopped
50 g (2 oz) pine kernels or slivered almonds
1 tablespoon chopped fresh parsley
salt and freshly ground black pepper

Heat the oil in a large pan, add the onion, garlic and ginger and cook for a few minutes until softened but not browned. Stir in the ground spices and the rice and cook for 1 minute, then stir in the stock and tomatoes. Add all the remaining ingredients and stir well. Cover and cook over a low-to-medium heat for about 20 minutes, until the rice is cooked, the liquid absorbed and the vegetables tender. Serve with warm pitta bread and a salad.

*Valerie Barrett*

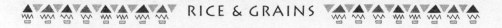 

# MILLET AND LENTIL BAKE

*Serves 4–6*

*Dishes with millet and lentils have been eaten in the Middle East for centuries. They are a good example of how people have combined two of their basic foods to provide a balanced meal -- without the guidance of modern nutritional science.*

2 tablespoons oil
1 onion, chopped
3 garlic cloves, crushed
250 g (8 oz) millet, soaked in cold water for 1 hour, then drained
1.5 litres ($2^1/_2$ pints) vegetable stock
6 cloves
seeds from 3 cardamom pods, crushed
$^1/_2$ teaspoon ground cinnamon
2 bay leaves
250 g (8 oz) red lentils
salt and freshly ground black pepper

Preheat the oven to 150°C (300°F, Gas Mark 2). Heat the oil in a heatproof casserole dish, add the onion and garlic and cook for a few minutes, until softened. Add the millet, stock, cloves, cardamom seeds, cinnamon and bay leaves and bring to the boil. Reduce the heat, cover and simmer very gently for 1 hour or until the millet is almost cooked. Add the lentils and cook for a further 15 minutes or until they are tender. Season to taste.

Pour off any remaining liquid, then replace the lid and transfer the dish to the oven. Bake for 10–20 minutes until the moisture has been absorbed; it should be a fairly dry mixture. Green salad makes a good accompaniment, together with cucumber raita – simply dice some cucumber and mix it with plain yogurt.

The Turkana people who live in northern Kenya are skilled at preparing food from the wild roots, berries and fruits that grow in even the driest areas. Some families also plant fast-growing crops such as millet and sorghum in places where rainfall collects – close to riverbeds or where the land dips.

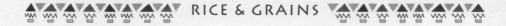 

# PEARL BARLEY 'RISOTTO'

*Serves 4*

*Unlike a traditional risotto, this is made with pearl barley, which is not only very nutritious but also delicious. My baby daughter Scarlett adores this, as do my two elder children. You could use a mixture of barley and rice if you like.*

1 onion, chopped
1 small red pepper, chopped
1 tablespoon olive oil
175 g (6 oz) pearl barley
600 ml (1 pint) vegetable stock
50 g (2 oz) brown cap (or button) mushrooms, stalks removed and sliced
salt and freshly ground black pepper

Sauté the onion and red pepper in the oil until softened. Add the barley and stir over a low heat for 2 minutes, then pour in the stock and bring to the boil. Reduce the heat and simmer uncovered, stirring occasionally, for about 35 minutes or until the barley is tender. Add the sliced mushrooms and continue to cook for 6–7 minutes. Season to taste and serve.

*Annabel Karmel*

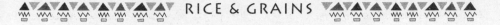
# BROWN RICE WITH CRISP VEGETABLES

*Serves 4*

1 onion, sliced
1 garlic clove, crushed
2 tablespoons olive oil
375 g (12 oz) brown rice
900 ml (1¹/₂ pints) hot vegetable stock
salt and freshly ground black pepper
1 small cauliflower, divided into florets
250 g (8 oz) carrots, diced
2 leeks, sliced
125 g (4 oz) peas
25 g (1 oz) butter
125 g (4 oz) Cheddar cheese, grated
1 tablespoon chopped fresh mint
1 tablespoon chopped fresh parsley
freshly grated Parmesan cheese, to serve (optional)

Fry the onion and garlic in the oil over a moderate heat for 2 minutes, stirring occasionally. Add the rice and cook for 1 minute. Pour in the hot stock, add salt and pepper and bring to the boil. Reduce the heat, cover and simmer for about 40 minutes, or until the rice is just tender and all the stock has been absorbed.

While the rice is cooking, steam the cauliflower, carrots and leeks for about 5 minutes, then add the peas and steam for a further 5 minutes, until the vegetables are almost tender but still crisp.

Melt the butter in a separate pan and fry the steamed vegetables in it for about 4–5 minutes, stirring frequently, until the vegetables are glazed with the butter but not browned. Stir the vegetables, Cheddar and mint into the cooked rice. Serve sprinkled with the parsley and with Parmesan, if liked.

*Odette Mansell, Guildford, Surrey*

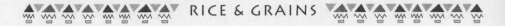 

# NASI GORENG

*Serves 2–4*

*This is a traditional Indonesian dish that can be eaten at any time of day and served hot or cold. It is particularly good with a fried egg on top.*

175 g (6 oz) long-grain rice
5 tablespoons vegetable oil
2 onions, chopped
2 garlic cloves, crushed
2 mild chillies (optional)
50–75 g (2–3 oz) cashew nuts, chopped
1 large carrot, finely diced
150 g (5 oz) fresh or frozen peas

Cook the rice according to the instructions on the packet. Meanwhile, heat 3 tablespoons of the oil in a pan, add the onions, garlic and the whole chillies, if using, and cook until soft and brown. Add the nuts, carrot and peas and cook for 8–10 minutes. Stir in the remaining oil, then when it is hot add the cooked rice and mix together well.

*Roberta Jordan, St Peter Port, Guernsey*

'I have my breakfast at 6 am during term-time. I have nasi goreng – fried rice with chopped vegetables and sometimes with a fried egg on top. At school we have a break from 9.30–10am, when we eat something like vegetable fritters or meatballs. At 12 o'clock I go home and have the midday meal of rice, spinach and vegetables cooked in sour broth.'

*Yatno, a 14-year-old boy in Bandung, Indonesia*

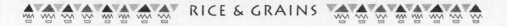 

# BRILLBURGERS

*Serves 6*

75 g (3 oz) breakfast wheat biscuits (3 biscuits)
75 g (3 oz) carrots, finely grated
75 g (3 oz) onions, finely grated
25 g (1 oz) almonds, finely chopped
25 g (1 oz) walnuts, finely chopped
50 g (2 oz) wholemeal flour
1 egg, beaten
salt and freshly ground black pepper
extra beaten egg and flour for coating
sunflower or vegetable oil for shallow-frying

Crumble the breakfast biscuits into a large bowl. Add the carrots, onions, nuts and flour and mix together thoroughly. Stir in the beaten egg and season with salt and pepper, then use your fingers to combine the ingredients, making sure the flour is thoroughly mixed in. Shape the mixture into burgers, dip each one into the extra beaten egg and then into flour to coat. Heat a thin layer of oil in a frying pan and fry the burgers over a gentle heat for about 3 minutes on each side, until golden brown. These burgers are delicious served with baked beans or a tomato sauce.

*Diane Louise Jordan*

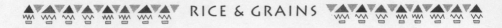 

# SPICY COCONUT RICE

*Serves 4*

*A good variation on this recipe is to use 3 tablespoons of peanut butter instead of coconut and make a spicy peanut rice.*

175 g (6 oz) basmati or plain rice
3 teaspoons soy sauce
2–3 tablespoons olive oil
1 large onion, finely chopped
3 garlic cloves, crushed
1 teaspoon finely chopped chilli
1 tablespoon finely grated fresh ginger root
1 green or red pepper, chopped
1 yellow pepper, chopped
125 g (4 oz) mushrooms, chopped
250 g (8 oz) broccoli, divided into florets
75 g (3 oz) creamed coconut

Cook the rice according to the instructions on the packet, adding the soy sauce to the water. Meanwhile, heat the olive oil in a pan and fry the onion and garlic until softened but not browned. Stir in the chilli and ginger and cook for a minute longer, then add all the remaining vegetables. Grate the creamed coconut into the mixture and stir until dissolved. Add a little water to stop the vegetables sticking. Cook, covered, for 5–10 minutes until the vegetables are tender. When the rice is cooked add it to the vegetables and stir.

*Veronica Armson, Greenwich, London*

'It takes a day to cycle to a village far away to buy coconuts for 200 *riels* (20p) each, then we bring them back to store outside our houses. Next day we take them to market to sell for 500 *riels*.'

*Kong Sophea, a Cambodian woman*

# PULSES

# CRISP TOFU WITH JAPANESE VEGETABLES AND MISO DIP

*Serves 2–4*

*In order to taste really good, tofu needs a crisp coating and a tasty sauce or marinade. Here it has both, served with a selection of pretty Japanese salads. Nori, anori ko and hiziki are all types of dried seaweed but if you can't get them, just leave them out.*

$1/_2$ cucumber, peeled and diced
1 bunch of radishes, sliced or cut into flowers
1 sheet of nori, 1 teaspoon of anori ko, or a few strands of hiziki
2 tablespoons rice vinegar
sugar and salt
1 carrot, cut into thin slices on the diagonal
6–8 baby sweetcorn, cut into thin slices on the diagonal
2 spring onions, cut into thin slices on the diagonal
2 teaspoons sesame seeds

*For the miso dip*
1 tablespoon miso – white, red or yellow
1 tablespoon soy sauce, preferably Kikkoman

*For the tofu*
groundnut oil for deep-frying
275 g (9 oz) block of firm tofu, cut into cubes
cornflour for coating

Put the cucumber and radishes in a bowl. If you are using nori, tear it into pieces and add to the bowl; just sprinkle in anori ko. For hiziki, simmer it in water for 5 minutes, then drain and add to the cucumber and radishes. Add half the rice vinegar and a little sugar and salt to taste.

Put the carrot, sweetcorn and spring onions in a separate bowl, sprinkle with the remaining rice vinegar and season with sugar and salt. Sprinkle the sesame seeds on top. Arrange the two salads on a serving platter. To make the dip, put the miso, soy sauce and 1 tablespoon of water into a small bowl and mix well.

Put the oil for frying on to heat: I use a medium-sized saucepan. Toss the tofu in the cornflour until thoroughly coated. When the oil is hot enough to bubble when a small crust of bread is thrown into it (or has reached 190°C/375°F) put in the tofu. You may need to cook it in 2 batches. When it is golden brown and crisp all over, remove it from the pan and drain on kitchen paper. Put the tofu on the platter of salads, along with the dip, and serve immediately.

*Rose Elliot*

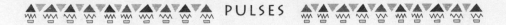 

# EASY D.I.Y. CHILLI

*Serves 2 ·*

*This is popular with most children and is an easy dish for older ones to make them-selves. It's good served with bread, a baked potato split and filled with yogurt or soured cream, some tortilla chips or some plain rice or pasta – and maybe a few salad leaves and some diced avocado.*

2 tablespoons vegetable oil
1 onion, chopped
1 small red or green pepper, chopped
1 carrot, coarsely grated or finely chopped
1 garlic clove, crushed
425g (15 oz) can of red kidney beans, drained
400g (13 oz) can of tomatoes
chilli powder, to taste
salt and freshly ground black pepper

Heat the oil in a saucepan and stir in the onion, pepper and carrot. Cover the pan and cook gently for 10 minutes, stirring occasionally, until the vegetables have softened slightly. Add the kidney beans and tomatoes, breaking up the tomatoes with a wooden spoon once they are in the pan. Bring to the boil, then cook over a moderate heat for about 10 minutes, until the mixture has lost its liquid appearance and the vegetables are tender. Stir in the chilli powder – start with a little, taste and add more until it is to your liking – and some salt and pepper. Cook for a few minutes longer and then serve.

*Rose Elliot*

The avocado is a rather expensive fruit in the UK
but in many parts of the world it is so cheap
and easily available that it is sometimes
called 'the butter of the poor'.

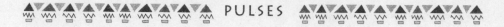 

# LENTIL AND WATERCRESS PATTIES

*Serves 4*

*These are delicious with mashed potatoes and a green vegetable.*

3 tablespoons oil
1 large onion, chopped
1 garlic clove, crushed
250 g (8 oz) red lentils, washed and drained
600 ml (1 pint) vegetable stock
2 tablespoons tomato purée
100 g ($3^1/_2$ oz) blanched almonds, chopped
1 bunch of watercress, finely chopped
1 tablespoon chopped fresh mint
salt and freshly ground black pepper
2 tablespoons plain flour
oil for shallow-frying

Heat the oil in a pan, add the onion and garlic and fry until softened but not browned. Add the lentils and stir to coat them with the oil, then pour in the stock and bring to the boil. Cover and simmer for about 40 minutes, or until the lentils are soft and all the stock has been absorbed. If there is still some liquid left, take the lid off the pan and increase the heat until it has evaporated. Beat the lentils with a wooden spoon until they turn into a rough purée and then beat in the tomato purée, almonds, watercress and mint. Season to taste.

Divide the mixture into 12 and shape into patties, then toss them in the flour to coat thoroughly. Shallow-fry them in hot oil over a moderate heat for about 5 minutes per side until crisp and brown. Serve hot or cold.

*Odette Mansell, Guildford, Surrey*

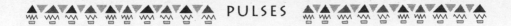
# LENTIL DELIGHT

*Serves 4*

*This is quick to put together for needy vegetarians when everyone else is having meat.*

250 g (8 oz) red lentils
400 g (13 oz) can of chopped tomatoes
1 tablespoon tomato purée
1 tablespoon vegetable oil
1 onion, chopped
1 teaspoon salt
$^1/_2$ teaspoon black pepper
450 ml ($^3/_4$ pint) vegetable stock or water
125 g (4 oz) cheese, grated

Preheat the oven to 190°C (375°F, Gas Mark 5). Mix together all the ingredients, reserving some of the cheese, and transfer to a greased shallow 25 cm (10 inch) heatproof dish. Bake, uncovered, for $1^1/_4$–$1^1/_2$ hours, stirring once or twice. Sprinkle over the remaining cheese before serving.

*Sally Coles, Church Enstone, Oxfordshire*

It's a staple food for about 200 million people. In the
developing world only rice, maize and sugar cane are
more important sources of calories. It's been called
'the greatest source of food energy in Africa'. Yet it is
known to most people in this country only in the form
of tapioca. What is this mystery crop?
Cassava, or manioc.

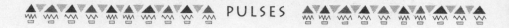
# CHEESY BEAN HOTPOT

*Serves 4*

2 tablespoons vegetable oil
1 large onion, chopped
2 celery sticks, chopped
2 carrots, chopped
3 garlic cloves, crushed
2 × 425 g (15 oz) cans of kidney beans, drained
400 g (13 oz) can of tomatoes
1 tablespoon tomato purée
2 tablespoons soy sauce
1 tablespoon chopped fresh parsley
125 g (4 oz) mature Cheddar cheese, grated

Heat the oil in a pan and cook the onion until softened. Add the celery, carrots and garlic and fry for 5 minutes. Stir in the beans, tomatoes, tomato purée and soy sauce. Cover tightly and simmer for about 45 minutes. Stir in the parsley, pour the mixture into a heatproof dish and sprinkle with the cheese. Place under a hot grill until golden brown, then serve with crusty bread.

*Elaine Brace, Cardiff*

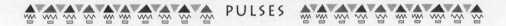
# MASALA WADA

*Serves 4*

*This dish has been popular in my country, Sri Lanka, for some time. It is crisp, tasty and nutritious.*

250 g (8 oz) yellow split peas, soaked overnight and drained
1 small onion, very finely chopped
$1/2$–1 teaspoon salt
$1/4$–$1/2$ teaspoon turmeric
1 green chilli, finely chopped (optional)
vegetable oil for deep-frying

Coarsely grind the soaked split peas (you can use a food processor for this). Do not add water. Mix with the onion, salt, turmeric and the chilli, if using. Shape into 2.5 cm (1 inch) balls and flatten them a little.

Heat the oil in a deep fryer or a saucepan and fry the balls a few at a time for 1–2 minutes, turning occasionally, until crisp and golden brown. Serve with chutney or with tomato or barbecue sauce.

*Malini Dissanayake, Oxfam volunteer, Newark, Nottinghamshire*

'Most days I walk into town with my mother – she sells peanuts in the park. We don't like Nairobi, we want to go back to our village. Mother says she will take us back when she has saved enough money.'

*Wangoi, a 10-year-old girl who came to Nairobi with her mother when her father died.*

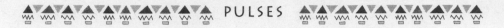 

# BLACK-EYED BEAN CASSEROLE

*Serves 4*

250 g (8 oz) black-eyed beans, soaked overnight
2 tablespoons olive oil
1 large onion, finely chopped
1 large garlic clove, finely chopped
600 ml (1 pint) dry cider
150 ml ($^1/_4$ pint) tomato passata
2 tablespoons tomato purée
1 tablespoon black treacle
1 tablespoon demerara sugar
1 teaspoon French mustard
salt and freshly ground black pepper
sprigs of parsley, to garnish

Drain the beans, rinse them thoroughly and place in a large saucepan. Cover with plenty of cold water, bring to the boil and boil steadily for 10 minutes, removing any scum with a slotted spoon. Reduce the heat, cover and simmer for 20 minutes, then drain.

Preheat the oven to 160°C (325°F, Gas Mark 3). Heat the oil in a pan, add the onion and garlic and fry gently until tender. Add the cider, passata, tomato purée, black treacle, sugar and mustard and bring to the boil, then remove from the heat.

Transfer the black-eyed beans to a casserole and add the prepared sauce. Stir well until evenly mixed, then cover and cook in the oven for $1^1/_2$–2 hours or until the beans are tender. Stir the beans occasionally and add a little extra cider or water if necessary to prevent them drying out. The finished sauce should be thick and soupy. Season with salt and pepper to taste.

Garnish with parsley sprigs and serve with hot crusty garlic bread or jacket potatoes and salad.

Potato Pizzas (page 132)

Crisp Tofu with Japanese Vegetables and Miso Dip (page 90)

Animal Pasta Salad with Multi-coloured Vegetables (page 74)

Refritos with Guacamole and Salsa (page 110)

Spicy Coconut Rice (page 88)

Vegetable Frittata (page 38)

*Above* Mixed Grain Wholemeal Loaf (page 172);
*Below* Broccoli and Sweetcorn Flan (page 50)

*Clockwise from left:* Carrot and Pineapple Muffins (page 166),
Chocolate Brownies (page 162), Quick Shortbread (page 168)

# AUBERGINE AND BEAN GRATIN

*Serves 4*

2 aubergines, ends trimmed
2 tablespoons olive oil
1 onion, chopped
1 garlic clove, crushed
125 g (4 oz) button mushrooms, halved
425 g (15 oz) can of cannellini beans, drained
2 tomatoes, chopped
freshly ground black pepper
2 level tablespoons freshly grated Parmesan cheese

Cook the aubergines in boiling water for about 10 minutes, until tender, then drain. Cut them in half lengthways and scoop out the flesh, leaving a 5 mm (¼ inch) shell. Finely chop the flesh.

Heat the oil in a frying pan, add the onion, garlic and chopped aubergine flesh and cook gently for 5 minutes. Add the mushrooms, beans, tomatoes and pepper to taste. Cook for a further 5 minutes, or until the mushrooms are tender. Stuff the aubergine shells with the mixture and sprinkle with the Parmesan cheese. Cook under a grill for 4–5 minutes or until heated through.

The aubergine has many different names, such as eggplant, apple of love, Jew's apple, widow's comforter, brown jolley and brinjal.

# TOFU BURGERS

*Makes 8*

300 g (10 oz) firm tofu
50 g (2 oz) cooked bulgur wheat or 125 g (4 oz) cooked rice
4 tablespoons hot water
1 onion, finely chopped
50 g (2 oz) mushrooms, finely chopped
50 g (2 oz) carrot, grated
1 vegetable stock cube, crushed
2 tablespoons soy sauce
2 teaspoons chopped fresh parsley
salt and freshly ground black pepper
2 tablespoons plain flour
oil for frying

Break the tofu into small pieces and put it in a bowl. Mix in all the remaining ingredients except the flour and oil and shape into burgers (the mixture may be sticky). Refrigerate for at least 1 hour, then coat the burgers lightly with the flour and shallow-fry in very hot oil for 3–4 minutes per side or until golden brown and heated through.

*Roberta Jordan, St Peter Port, Guernsey*

Over half the world's soya beans are grown in the USA. They are wonderful beans: a good source of protein and full of oil that can be used in cooking, soap, paint and plastics. They are available fresh, fermented or dried; the flour is used for baking and ice cream; soya milk can be drunk by people who are allergic to dairy products; and, of course, Chinese cooking wouldn't taste the same without soy sauce.

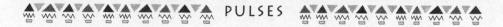 

# LENTIL AND CHEESE BAKE

*Serves 4*

750 ml (1¼ pints) water
250 g (8 oz) red lentils
1 onion, finely sliced
1 tablespoon finely chopped fresh parsley
1 garlic clove, crushed
1 celery stick, chopped
25 g (1 oz) butter or margarine
2 tablespoons plain flour
salt and freshly ground black pepper
2 tablespoons tomato purée
200 g (7 oz) Cheddar cheese, grated

Preheat the oven to 180°C (350°F, Gas Mark 4). Put the water in a saucepan and bring it to the boil. Add the lentils, onion, parsley, garlic and celery. Cover the pan, reduce the heat and simmer for about 15 minutes, until everything is tender. Pour off excess liquid and reserve. Spoon the lentil mixture into a greased ovenproof dish. Make up the reserved liquid to 300 ml (½ pint) with water.

Melt the butter or margarine in a pan. Sieve in the flour and mix well, then gradually add the liquid, stirring all the time, until the sauce thickens. Season with salt and pepper, then pour the sauce over the lentil mixture. Cover with the tomato purée, spreading this as evenly as possible. Sprinkle the grated cheese on top and bake for 10–15 minutes until the cheese is melted and bubbling.

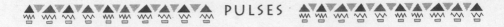 

# SPICED PINTO BEANS IN COCONUT MILK

*Serves 4*

2 tablespoons vegetable oil
1 onion, chopped
250 g (8 oz) pinto beans, cooked
3 tomatoes, chopped
$1^1/_2$ teaspoons turmeric
1 teaspoon chilli powder
salt
1 tablespoon chopped fresh coriander or parsley
350 ml (12 fl oz) coconut milk

Heat the oil in a deep, heavy pan and cook the onion gently until soft and golden. Partially mash the beans with a fork and then spoon them into the pan. Add the chopped tomatoes and mix well, then stir in the turmeric, chilli powder, salt and half the coriander or parsley. Pour in the coconut milk, then cover and simmer for 10 minutes. Garnish with the remaining coriander or parsley and serve with rice.

Collecting coconuts can be a bit of a problem. You could wait for them to fall but then they may be overripe, so the best method is to climb the tall trunk and cut them down. In some parts of Southeast Asia, monkeys have been trained to do this.

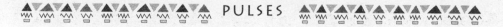 

# BLACK-EYED BEAN STEW

*Serves 4*

*These creamy white beans, with their black 'eye', are a staple food in parts of Africa and are also widely eaten in India.*

250 g (8 oz) black-eyed beans, cooked
1–2 tablespoons vegetable oil
1 onion, sliced
2 tomatoes, chopped
$^1/_2$ chilli, chopped, or $^1/_2$ teaspoon chilli powder
salt and freshly ground black pepper

Mash the cooked beans and set aside. Heat the oil in a pan and fry the onion and tomatoes for a few minutes until softened. Add the mashed beans, chilli and seasoning and cook for 10 minutes. Stir from time to time and add a little water if it becomes too dry. Serve hot with mashed yams, fried plantains or rice.

# RED BEAN AND RICE SALAD

*Serves 4*

175 g (6 oz) canned kidney beans
125 g (4 oz) sweetcorn
250 g (8 oz) cooked long-grain rice
1 garlic clove, crushed
a pinch of salt
a pinch of ground ginger
salad dressing, to taste

Put the kidney beans, sweetcorn, rice and garlic in a bowl and mix together. Add salt and ginger to taste, then toss with your favourite salad dressing.

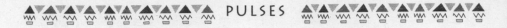 

# MUNG BEANS IN COCONUT MILK

*Serves 4*

*This is made with mung dal, the hulled, split form of mung beans, which should be available from healthfood shops or Indian grocers.*

250 g (8 oz) mung dal, cooked
salt
1 tablespoon vegetable oil
1 onion, sliced
200 ml (7 fl oz) coconut milk
$1/4$ teaspoon paprika
slices of red pepper, to garnish

Season the cooked mung dal with salt to taste and partially mash with a fork; set aside.

Heat the oil in a heavy pan and sauté the onion until soft. Gradually pour in the coconut milk and bring slowly to the boil, stirring well. Add the dal and stir to combine, then add the paprika and check the seasoning. Garnish with red pepper and serve with rice or mashed sweet potatoes.

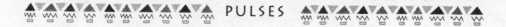 

# BEANS AND CORN

*Serves 4–6*

2 tablespoons vegetable oil
1 onion, chopped
3 red peppers, chopped
4 tomatoes, sliced
250 g (8 oz) black-eyed beans, cooked
300 g (11 oz) canned sweetcorn, drained
salt and freshly ground black pepper
1 teaspoon paprika

Heat the oil in a pan, add the onion and cook until softened. Add the peppers and cook for a few minutes, then stir in the tomatoes.

Mix the cooked beans and corn together in a bowl and add salt to taste. Add this mixture to the pan and season with pepper. Mix well, cover and cook for about 15 minutes, adding a little water if required as the dish should be moist. Serve with rice and a green vegetable or salad.

Corn comes in many colours – yellow, blue, black, red or a mixture.

# DAL WITH COCONUT

*Serves 4*

*This is delicious served with boiled rice that has had a handful of raisins and peas added to it to cook for the last 5 minutes.*

250 g (8 oz) red lentils
600 ml (1 pint) water
$1/_2$ teaspoon turmeric
1 teaspoon coarsely chopped fresh ginger root
$1/_2$ onion, chopped
salt and freshly ground black pepper
15 g ($1/_2$ oz) butter or margarine
3 tablespoons desiccated coconut

Put the lentils and water in a pan and bring to the boil, skimming off any froth that rises to the surface. Add the turmeric, ginger and onion and simmer for 10 minutes or until the lentils are almost tender and the water has been almost completely absorbed. Season and continue to cook until the lentils are tender.

Meanwhile, melt the butter or margarine in a pan and stir in the coconut. Cook gently, stirring, until the coconut turns a rich brown colour. When the dal is ready, spoon it into a serving dish and sprinkle the hot coconut over it.

# QUICK BEANS WITH CRUNCHY TOPPING

*Serves 4*

*This recipe has been adapted from 'Blue Peter'. You can swap curried beans, chick peas, green peas or broad beans for any of the canned ingredients, or substitute peppers, aubergines or courgettes for any of the fresh ingredients. The beans are also good topped with lightly toasted French bread slices spread with a little butter and wholegrain mustard, then sprinkled with the cheese.*

vegetable oil for frying
1 onion, sliced
2 tomatoes, chopped
125 g (4 oz) mushrooms, chopped
425 g (15 oz) can of baked beans
425 g (15 oz) can of kidney beans, drained
200 g (7 oz) can of sweetcorn, drained
1 tablespoon tomato purée
2–3 slices of bread
125 g (4 oz) cheese, grated

Heat a little oil in a large frying pan, add the onion, tomatoes and mushrooms and cook gently until tender. Stir in all the beans, the sweetcorn and tomato purée and continue to cook gently until everything is thoroughly heated through, stirring occasionally

Transfer the mixture to a large heatproof dish. Tear up the slices of bread and place them on top of the bean mixture. Cover with the grated cheese and place under a hot grill until the cheese melts.

*Vivienne Wright, Oxfam volunteer, Grays Thurrock, Essex*

# RED DRAGON PIE

*Serves 4*

*This is a lovely recipe for a cold, wintry day – a superior shepherd's pie with an appealing name for children.*

125 g (4 oz) aduki beans, soaked overnight and drained
50 g (2 oz) brown or white rice, washed and drained
1 tablespoon vegetable oil
1 onion, chopped
250 g (8 oz) carrots, diced
1–2 tablespoons soy sauce
2 tablespoons tomato purée
1 teaspoon dried mixed herbs
500 g (1 lb potatoes), diced
40 g (1$^1/_2$ oz) butter or margarine
a little milk
salt and freshly ground black pepper

Rinse the aduki beans and put them in a pan with 1.2 litres (2 pints) of water. Bring to the boil, then reduce the heat and cook for 50 minutes or until tender. Drain and reserve 300 ml ($^1/_2$ pint) of the cooking liquid. Cook the rice in a separate pan until tender, then drain.

Preheat the oven to 180°C (350°F, Gas Mark 4). Heat the oil in a saucepan and fry the onion for 5 minutes, until softened, then add the carrots and cook for 2–3 minutes. Stir in the cooked beans and rice. Mix the soy sauce, tomato purée and herbs with the reserved cooking liquid and add to the pan. Bring to the boil, cover and simmer for 20–30 minutes.

Meanwhile, boil the potatoes until tender, then drain and mash with 25 g (1 oz) of the butter or margarine, the milk and plenty of seasoning.

Season the bean mixture to taste and add more liquid if necessary so that it is moist. Transfer to a greased ovenproof dish, spread the mashed potatoes over the top, dot with the remaining butter or margarine and bake for 35–40 minutes or until the topping is crisp and brown. Serve with green vegetables.

*Sylvia Wade, Oxfam volunteer, Grays Thurrock, Essex*

# DUTCH STAMPPOT

*Serves 4*

*For a really tasty topping, try adding some grated cheese to the mashed potatoes.*

1 tablespoon sunflower oil
1 onion, finely chopped
4 celery sticks, diced
250 g (8 oz) carrots, diced
425 g (15 oz) can of butterbeans, drained
400 g (13 oz) can of tomatoes, puréed, or passata
1 bay leaf
1 teaspoon dried thyme or dried mixed herbs
2 tablespoons finely chopped fresh parsley
1 teaspoon yeast extract, dissolved in 150 ml ($1/_4$ pint) hot water
salt and freshly ground black pepper
500 g (1 lb) potatoes, cooked and mashed

Preheat the oven to 180°C (350°F, Gas Mark 4). Heat the oil in a pan and gently fry the onion for 3–4 minutes, until softened. Add the celery, carrots and butterbeans. Cook for 5 minutes, then stir in the puréed tomatoes or passata, all the herbs and the dissolved yeast extract. Bring to the boil, cover and simmer for 20 minutes, then season to taste.

Transfer the mixture to a lightly greased ovenproof dish, cover with the mashed potatoes and bake in the oven for 15–20 minutes.

*Lucy Day, Horsham, West Sussex*

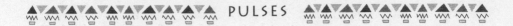 

# SOYA BEAN CUTLETS

*Serves 6–8*

vegetable oil for frying
125 g (4 oz) onions, finely diced
2 chillies or 1 small pepper, finely diced (optional)
6 garlic cloves, crushed to a paste
1 teaspoon white pepper
1 teaspoon chilli powder
salt
425 g (15 oz) can of soya beans, drained and mashed
375 g (12 oz) potatoes, boiled and mashed
125 g (4 oz) cheese, grated
juice of $1/_2$ lime, or to taste
1–2 eggs, beaten
breadcrumbs for coating
lettuce leaves, to serve

Heat 2 tablespoons of vegetable oil in a wok or large frying pan and add the onions, chillies or pepper, if using, and garlic. When they turn brown, stir in the white pepper, chilli powder and salt, then add the soya beans and potatoes. Mix well, remove from the heat and add the grated cheese and lime juice to taste.

Shape the mixture into 18 small cutlets, flattening them slightly. Dip them in the beaten egg and then in breadcrumbs, pressing them on well. Heat a thin layer of vegetable oil in a pan and shallow-fry the cutlets for 3–4 minutes per side or until golden brown and heated through (or you can deep-fry them for 1–2 minutes per side). Serve on a bed of lettuce.

*Deepthi de Silva, Colombo, Sri Lanka*

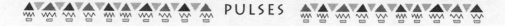
# IRIO

*Serves 8*

500 g (1 lb) kidney beans, soaked overnight and drained
500 g (1 lb) potatoes, diced
250 g (8 oz) canned sweetcorn, drained
125 g (4 oz) spinach, chopped
salt and freshly ground black pepper
50 g (2 oz) butter, diced
3 tablespoons cream

Bring 1 litre ($1^3/_4$ pints) of water to the boil in a large pan, then add the kidney beans. Boil hard for 10 minutes, then reduce the heat to a simmer and cook for 45 minutes or until tender. Add the potatoes and cook for 15 minutes, then add the sweetcorn and spinach and cook for a few more minutes, until everything is tender. Season with salt and pepper.

Thoroughly drain the vegetables and place them in a dish, then stir in the butter and cream. Mash the vegetables with a fork and serve straight away.

Arfaza Begum lives on an island in Bangladesh.
She doesn't have a job. 'I have to go round the
neighbours every day asking for food. They usually
give me something, a few *taka* (62 *taka* = £1) or a
handful of rice. I haven't eaten today.'

# REFRITOS WITH GUACAMOLE AND SALSA

*Serves 4*

*Refritos means refried beans, which are very popular in Mexico as are guacamole and salsa. Try filling fresh tortillas with these sizzling stuffings.*

25 g (1 oz) butter or margarine
1 onion, chopped
1 garlic clove, crushed
425 g (15 oz) can of red kidney beans, drained
a pinch of chilli powder
soured cream, to serve

*For the guacamole*
2 ripe avocados, peeled and stoned
juice of $^1/_2$ lemon
1 tomato, skinned and chopped
1 spring onion, finely chopped
3 tablespoons soured cream
a pinch of salt
a pinch of chilli powder
sprigs of coriander or parsley, to garnish (optional)

*For the salsa*
400 g (13 oz) can of chopped tomatoes or 500 g (1 lb) fresh ripe tomatoes,
skinned and chopped
1 small onion, finely chopped
$^1/_2$ teaspoon chilli powder, or to taste
a pinch of sugar
salt and freshly ground black pepper
2 tablespoons chopped fresh coriander or parsley (optional)

Melt the butter or margarine in a pan over a medium heat and fry the onion and garlic gently for 5 minutes, until softened. Mash the kidney beans and add them to the mixture with the chilli powder. Cook for a few minutes until hot.

To make the guacamole, mix all the ingredients together, either in a blender or food processor or by mashing them up with a fork. To make the salsa, simply combine all the ingredients in a bowl.

Serve the beans topped with soured cream and accompanied by the guacamole and salsa, plus warm tortillas or pitta bread, if liked.

# VEGETABLES & NUTS

# POTATO CAKES WITH TOFU

*Serves 2*

*Nutritionally, tofu is a wonder food, virtually fat-free and high in protein, calcium and iron. I also like the fact that it has been made for thousands of years rather than being a novelty 'health food' of dubious merit. However, it does need jazzing up in order to taste good. Here is one way which is popular with children of all ages: an old favourite, potato cakes, made into a main course with the addition of tofu – rather like fish cakes, perhaps. (For another good way to prepare tofu, see page 90.)*

250 g (8 oz) potatoes, diced
15 g ($^{1}/_{2}$ oz) butter or margarine
125 g (4 oz) firm tofu
1 tablespoon finely chopped onion or spring onion
1–2 tablespoons chopped fresh parsley or chives
salt and freshly ground black pepper
flour for coating
oil for shallow-frying

Boil the potatoes until tender, then drain and mash with the butter or margarine. Add the tofu, onion and herbs and mash well to make a smooth mixture. Season with salt and pepper, then shape into flat cakes and coat with flour. Heat a thin layer of oil in a frying pan and fry the cakes until crisp and golden brown, turning them to cook both sides.

*Rose Elliot*

Fancy a freeze-dried potato? They're popular in the
Altiplano of Peru, where the icy winds at night
literally freeze-dry the small potatoes known
as *chuno*. They keep well, taste good in
stews and can be ground into a flour.

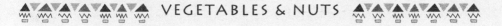 

# HEALTHY HOME-MADE OVEN CHIPS

*Serves 2–4*

*Potatoes are a good food for children and I think that chips have an unnecessarily bad press considering the nutrients they contain. Still, I can't deny that most chips are rather high in fat. The same cannot be said of these, which are a surprisingly good substitute.*

500 g (1 lb) waxy potatoes
1 tablespoon oil

Preheat the oven to 200°C (400°F, Gas Mark 6). Peel the potatoes and cut them into fairly thick chips. Sprinkle the oil over them, turning them with your fingers so that they are all coated with it. Spread them out in a single layer on a baking sheet and bake for about 35 minutes, then turn them over and cook for a further 10 minutes of so, until they are crisp and golden brown.

*Rose Elliot*

Harvest is a time of celebration for people throughout the world, when the fruits of their labours are finally realized. In Ecuador, harvest coincides with the longest days of the year and people enjoy the 'Inti Raymi', or Festival of the Sun. Everyone dresses up and takes to the streets, singing and dancing.

# MAGIC CIRCLES

*Makes 2*

*These almond circles are almost like crisp savoury biscuits but they make a nutritious main course – and disappear like magic! They are good served with very light, creamy mashed potato – the circles can be used to scoop it up, like eating a dip. Or you can make them into nests by putting some mashed potato on top, hollowing out the centre of the potato slightly and topping with a few vegetables, such as sweetcorn, baby Brussels sprouts or broccoli florets, to be 'eggs in the nest'.*

1 Weetabix
25 g (1 oz) flaked almonds
2 teaspoons very finely chopped or grated onion
15 g (¹/₂ oz) butter, softened
salt and freshly ground black pepper

Preheat the oven to 200°C (400°F, Gas Mark 6). Crumble the Weetabix into a bowl, then add the rest of the ingredients and mix them together well with your fingers, scrunching up the nuts a bit. Add 1 teaspoon of cold water to make a dough that just holds together. Divide into 2 equal pieces and put them on a lightly greased baking sheet. Press each one down firmly into a circle, making it as thin as you can. The circles can be close together as they won't spread. Bake for 5–8 minutes or until they are crisp and beginning to brown at the edges. Cool very slightly, then lift them carefully off the baking sheet with a fish slice.

*Rose Elliot*

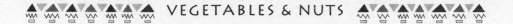 

# STIR-FRIED CABBAGE WITH COCONUT

*Serves 4*

*This recipe was passed down by my mother and I have passed it on to my daughters and granddaughter, who love it. It is delicious served with bread, rice or pancakes, and is also very good made with spinach instead of cabbage.*

$1/2$ large cabbage, finely chopped
1 tablespoon vegetable oil
$1/2$ onion, finely chopped
1 small green chilli, deseeded and finely chopped
1 tablespoon desiccated coconut
salt

Cook the cabbage in a little water over a low heat for a few minutes until tender, then drain. In a separate pan, heat the oil and fry the onion and chilli until softened. Stir in the cabbage and desiccated coconut, add salt to taste, then serve.

*Mrs Q. Hopwood, Rotherham, South Yorkshire*

In addition to their wealth of uses, coconut palms are
a good source of income, because they can be grown
by the coast in salty and sandy soils where other
plants wither and die

# SPINACH TORTILLAS

*Serves 4*

*I invented this dish after assimilating a few recipes from a Mexican cookbook and finding that I had these ingredients in my fridge. Serve with tomatoes or tomato sauce and avocado mashed with soured cream.*

1 large onion, chopped
1–3 garlic cloves, crushed
1 large red pepper, chopped
125 g (4 oz) mushrooms, chopped
125 g (4 oz) cabbage, chopped
500 g (1 lb) spinach, chopped
2 teaspoons ground coriander
1 tablespoon tomato purée
salt and freshly ground black pepper
125 g (4 oz) Cheddar cheese, grated
8 fresh tortillas (wheat or corn)

Preheat the oven to 180°C (350°F, Gas Mark 4). Fry the onion, garlic, pepper, mushrooms and cabbage until softened. Add the spinach and cook until wilted, then stir in the coriander and tomato purée and season to taste. Remove from the heat and add the grated cheese.

Divide the filling between the tortillas and roll them up. Place them side by side in a greased ovenproof dish, cover with foil and bake in the oven for 20–30 minutes.

*Belinda Lang*

That's a-maize-ing.
We tend to call it corn but in South Africa it is mealie.
In many parts of Latin America and Africa maize is the
staple food, eaten in many different ways: *ugali* is an
East African maize porridge; the Algonquin Indians of
North America call their maize bread *pone*; in Peru it is
toasted as *cancha*, or boiled to make *mote*; tortillas are
maize cakes from Latin America.

# CARROT CRUMBLE

*Serves 4*

500 g (1 lb) carrots
15 g ($^{1}/_{2}$ oz) butter
2 teaspoons clear honey
3 tablespoons vegetable stock
salt and freshly ground black pepper
250 g (8 oz) canned sweetcorn, drained
1 tablespoon chopped fresh parsley

*For the topping*
125 g (4 oz) wholemeal flour
$^{1}/_{2}$ teaspoon salt
65 g ($2^{1}/_{2}$ oz) butter or margarine
25 g (1 oz) breadcrumbs
a pinch of ground ginger

Preheat the oven to 190°C (375°F, Gas Mark 5). Cook the carrots in boiling salted water until tender, then drain and slice them into a bowl. Stir in the butter, honey and stock and season to taste. Arrange them in a greased 1 litre ($1^{3}/_{4}$ pint) ovenproof dish, cover with the sweetcorn and sprinkle over the parsley.

To make the topping, sift the flour and salt into a bowl and rub in the butter or margarine. Stir in the breadcrumbs and ginger. Cover the vegetables with the topping and bake in the oven for 20 minutes or until the topping is crisp and brown.

*Odette Mansell, Guildford, Surrey*

# POTATO PANCAKES WITH CARROT AND COURGETTE

*Makes about 12*

1 small onion, grated
1 small (75 g/3 oz) carrot, finely grated
1 small (75 g/3 oz) courgette, finely grated
1 baking potato (250 g/8 oz), peeled, coarsely grated and
squeezed dry in a tea towel
2 eggs
2 tablespoons plain flour
salt and freshly ground black pepper
vegetable oil for frying

Put the onion, carrot, courgette and potato in a bowl. Beat together the eggs, flour and seasoning, add to the vegetables and stir very well together.

Heat a griddle or heavy-based frying pan and brush with oil. Put large spoonfuls of the vegetable mixture on to the hot griddle or pan and spread each one slightly to make 8–10 cm (3–4 inch) pancakes. Cook for about 3–4 minutes, until golden brown underneath, and then flip them over and cook the other side for 3–4 minutes. Serve with tomato ketchup or a spicy sauce.

*Valerie Barrett*

# WILD MUSHROOM BURGERS

*Serves 4*

*Oyster, shiitake, chanterelle or cep mushrooms can be used for this recipe, or a combination. Most of these mushrooms are readily available in supermarkets nowadays or you can pick your own wild mushrooms, but always have them identified by an expert before you cook them.*

250 g (8 oz) wild mushrooms
1 onion
2 teaspoons finely chopped fresh tarragon or parsley
2 teaspoons ground cumin
50 g (2 oz) wholemeal flour
1 egg, beaten
3 garlic cloves, finely chopped
75 g (3 oz) fresh breadcrumbs
1 teaspoon lemon juice
1 hard-boiled egg, mashed
2 teaspoons freshly grated Parmesan cheese
salt and freshly ground black pepper
2 tablespoons extra virgin olive oil

*For the coating*
1 egg, beaten
125 g (4 oz) medium oatmeal

Chop the mushrooms and onion very finely in a food processor, then put them in a large bowl and mix with the tarragon or parsley and cumin. Stir in the flour then add the egg to bind the mixture; it should be quite stiff, so you may not need all the egg. Add all the remaining ingredients except the olive oil and mix well, then shape into 8–10 burgers. Dip them in the beaten egg and coat with the oatmeal.

Heat the olive oil in a large frying pan and fry the burgers until golden brown and cooked through. Serve with baked potatoes and salad.

*Tom Whitaker (aged 12), Whitstable, Kent*

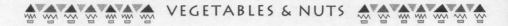

# AUBREY AUBERGINE

*Serves 4*

1 large aubergine, sliced (peel first for very young children)
salt and freshly ground black pepper
3–4 tomatoes, sliced
175–250g (6–8 oz) cheese, grated
1–2 tablespoons olive oil

Preheat the oven to 200°C (400°F, Gas Mark 6). Sprinkle the aubergine slices with a little salt and leave to stand for about 30 minutes, then rinse thoroughly. Cut one of the larger slices in half and reserve one of the halves.

Set 2 even-sized tomato slices aside, then layer the aubergine, tomatoes and cheese in a casserole dish, seasoning each layer with a little black pepper and finishing with a layer of cheese. Place the reserved tomato slices on top for Aubrey's eyes and use the half slice of aubergine for a mouth. Trickle the olive oil over the top and bake in the oven for 30 minutes. Serve with baked potatoes or rice.

*Mrs M. Smith, Normanton, West Yorkshire*

# POTATO CAKES WITH PEANUT SAUCE AND POACHED EGGS

*Serves 6*

*This is from Ecuador and it brings together some of that country's staple foods – potatoes, eggs and peanuts – into a favourite dish.*

25 g (1 oz) butter or margarine
2 onions, finely chopped
1 kg (2 lb) potatoes, cooked and mashed
2 tablespoons chopped fresh parsley
200 g (7 oz) Cheddar cheese, grated
salt and freshly ground black pepper
vegetable oil for frying
125 g (4 oz) peanut butter
125 ml (4 fl oz) vegetable stock or water
a squeeze of lemon juice
6 eggs
a few lettuce leaves

Melt the butter or margarine in a pan and cook the onions in it until they are soft and golden. Transfer them to a bowl and stir in the mashed potatoes, parsley and cheese, adding salt and pepper to taste. Shape this mixture into cakes about 2.5 cm (1 inch) thick. Heat a little oil in a frying pan and when it is very hot, add the potato cakes. Fry until golden on one side and then turn them over to cook the other side. Keep the potato cakes warm while you prepare the sauce and eggs.

To make the sauce, put the peanut butter and stock or water into a small saucepan and heat gently, stirring to combine. Add a squeeze of lemon juice and season to taste.

Poach the eggs, then place the potato cakes on a dish lined with lettuce leaves, slide the eggs on top and pass the peanut sauce round separately.

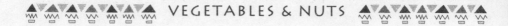
# CHEESE AND POTATO CAKE

*Serves 2*

500 g (1 lb) potatoes, boiled and mashed
50 g (2 oz) Cheddar cheese, grated
1 heaped tablespoon plain flour
salt and freshly ground black pepper

Put all the ingredients into a bowl and mix well together, then form into rounds. Transfer to a lightly greased baking tray and place under a preheated grill until nicely browned and heated through, turning to cook the other side. Serve with a poached egg on top of each cake and some baked beans. For an older child, you could add some shredded lettuce and sliced tomatoes.

*Margery Rook, Blackpool, Lancashire*

# PUMPKIN AU GRATIN

*Serves 4*

50 g (2 oz) butter
2 kg (4$^1$/$_2$ lb) pumpkin, peeled and diced
150 ml ($^1$/$_4$ pint) double cream
salt and freshly ground black pepper
grated cheese and breadcrumbs, for sprinkling

Preheat the oven to 200°C (400°F, Gas Mark 6). Heat half the butter in a pan, add the pumpkin and cook gently, covered, for 30 minutes, stirring occasionally to prevent sticking. When the pumpkin is tender, drain thoroughly.

Heat the remaining butter in a pan, add the pumpkin and cream and mash thoroughly with a fork. Season well. Pour into a greased soufflé dish, sprinkle with cheese and breadcrumbs and bake in the oven for 30 minutes, until golden brown.

# VEGGIE STEW

*Serves 4*

*Grandma made up this recipe for Alex (aged 7) who is vegetarian, using ingredients he likes to eat.*

1 large onion, chopped
3 celery sticks, chopped
3 carrots, sliced
500–750 g (1–1$^1/_2$ lb) potatoes, diced
150 ml ($^1/_4$ pint) vegetable stock
200 g (7 oz) can of kidney beans, drained
425 g (14 oz) can of ratatouille
salt and freshly ground black pepper
a dash of vegetarian Worcestershire sauce

Cook the onion, celery and carrots in boiling salted water until tender, then drain. Cook the potatoes in a separate pan until tender, then drain. Put all the cooked vegetables in a pan, add the vegetable stock and simmer for 5 minutes. Add the kidney beans, ratatouille, seasoning and Worcestershire sauce. Heat gently without letting it boil.

*Dorothy Bradbury, Old Trafford, Manchester*

# FRUIT CURRY

*Serves 6*

*I invented this recipe as I am not too fond of meaty and extremely spicy curries. Children like it and the varied fruit content is easy for them to digest.*

3 baking potatoes, diced
1 onion, chopped
375 g (12 oz) cooking apples or Granny Smiths, peeled, cored and diced
1 large banana, chopped
2–3 carrots, sliced
400 g (13 oz) can of chopped tomatoes
425 g (14 oz) can of pineapple pieces in natural juice
250 g (8 oz) mango chutney
500 g (1 lb) yogurt
2 tablespoons mild curry powder
2 tablespoons tikka paste
40 g (1 1/2 oz) shredded or desiccated coconut
2 garlic cloves, crushed

Simply put all the ingredients in a large saucepan and simmer over a low heat for 2–3 hours. Remove the lid for the last 30 minutes if there is too much liquid. Serve on a bed of mixed rice and peas, garnished with a few bay leaves.

*Michelle Scully, Aylesbury, Buckinghamshire*

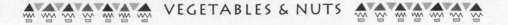 

# PAN HAGGERTY

*Serves 2–3*

*This is a traditional dish from the north of England.*

25 g (1 oz) butter
625 g (1¼ lb) potatoes, thinly sliced
salt and freshly ground black pepper
2 large onions, thinly sliced
75–125 g (3–4 oz) mature Cheddar or Cheshire cheese, grated
chopped fresh parsley, to garnish

Melt the butter in a large heavy frying pan. Arrange overlapping layers of potatoes in the pan, seasoning between the layers, then arrange the onions over the top, season and sprinkle with the grated cheese. Cover with a lid and cook over a moderate heat for 35–40 minutes, until the vegetables are tender. Check the potatoes at the bottom occasionally; they should form a golden brown crust. Place under a preheated grill to brown the cheese, then sprinkle with parsley and serve straight from the pan, cut into wedges.

*Jane Middleton*

An evening meal of *injera*, a pancake-like bread made from sorghum, served with a spicy sauce of boiled cabbage and potato, is eaten at dusk in Ethiopia. The next morning it is chopped up and lightly cooked in a watery *wat*, thickened with a little sweet potato, for breakfast.

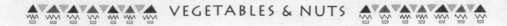 

# NUT ROAST

*Serves 4*

1 oz (25 g) butter or margarine
1 onion, finely chopped
250 g (8 oz) mixed nuts, such as walnuts, cashews,
brazils, pecans, almonds and hazelnuts
125 g (4 oz) wholemeal breadcrumbs
300 ml ($^1/_2$ pint) strong vegetable stock, warmed
1 teaspoon mixed herbs
1 egg, beaten (optional)
salt and freshly ground black pepper

Preheat the oven to 180°C (350°F, Gas Mark 4). Heat the butter or margarine in a pan and cook the onion until soft. Grind the nuts and breadcrumbs together in a food processor or blender, reserving about a tablespoon of the breadcrumbs, then combine with all the other ingredients. Turn into a greased ovenproof dish and sprinkle with the remaining breadcrumbs. Bake for 30 minutes, until set and brown. This mixture can also be used to make rissoles.

*Ida McCabe, Tavistock, Devon*

# ANNABEL'S MINESTRONE

*Serves 4*

*This main-course soup is a very versatile recipe as you can add rice, pasta and almost any vegetable. I've even been known to add a can of novelty-shaped pasta such as Thomas the Tank Engine at the very end instead of the dried pasta shapes, which will give the minestrone guaranteed child appeal!*

15 g (½ oz) butter or margarine
½ small onion, chopped
1 carrot, chopped
½ celery stalk, chopped
½ white of leek, chopped
125 g (4 oz) cabbage, shredded
1.75 litres (3 pints) vegetable stock
1 potato, diced
1 tablespoon chopped fresh parsley
2 teaspoons tomato purée
50 g (2 oz) small pasta shapes
125 g (4 oz) peas

Melt the butter or margarine in a pan and sauté the onion for a couple of minutes, then add the carrot, celery and leek. Sauté these for 2 minutes, then add the cabbage and continue to cook for another 4 minutes. Pour in the stock. Add the potato, parsley and tomato purée, then bring to the boil. Reduce the heat, cover and cook over a gentle heat for 20–25 minutes. Add the pasta and peas about 8 minutes prior to the end of cooking.

*Annabel Karmel*

# EASY-PEASY JAPANESY

*Serves 1*

1 tablespoon olive oil
2 tomatoes, quartered
50 g (2 oz) mushrooms, sliced if large
2 small potatoes, quartered and boiled for 8 minutes
2 celery sticks, sliced
1 small onion, chopped
1 garlic clove, crushed
salt and freshly ground black pepper
50 g (2 oz) fresh breadcrumbs
50 g (2 oz) full-flavoured cheese, grated

Heat the olive oil in a heavy-based pan, add the vegetables and cook gently for 10 minutes or until tender, stirring occasionally to prevent the vegetables sticking. Season to taste and spoon into a heatproof dish. Mix together the breadcrumbs and cheese, spread on top of the vegetables and place under a hot grill, until golden brown.

*Kay Cartwright, Sittingbourne, Kent*

# CORN FRITTERS

*Serves 4*

*In Thailand, vendors sell little fritters like these from stalls along the street.*

325 g (11 oz) canned sweetcorn, drained
1 onion, finely chopped
$1/2$ teaspoon chilli powder
2 garlic cloves, finely chopped
4 spring onions, finely chopped
1 teaspoon ground coriander
3 tablespoons plain flour
1 teaspoon baking powder
a pinch of salt
1 egg
4 tablespoons olive oil

Crush the sweetcorn for a few seconds in a blender or food processor. Transfer to a bowl and mix with all the remaining ingredients except the oil. Heat the oil in a frying pan, and drop in spoonfuls of the mixture to make fritters. Fry gently for 3 minutes, or until golden underneath, then turn over and cook for a further 2–3 minutes. Drain on kitchen paper and serve them while they're hot.

# ITALIAN GRILLED VEGETABLES

*Serves 2–4*

*These can be eaten either hot or cold. If you serve them hot, make some bread croûtons to put them on. Spread 4 slices of brown bread generously with butter on both sides, then heat a little olive oil and fry until golden brown. Alternatively, make a grilled vegetable sandwich with delicious ciabatta bread.*

1 aubergine, cut lengthways into strips about 5 mm ($^1/_4$ inch) thick
3 courgettes, cut lengthways into strips about 5 mm ($^1/_4$ inch) thick
4 tomatoes, cut in half
6 mushrooms, sliced into 3 or 4 pieces
1 red, green or yellow pepper, sliced
salt and freshly ground black pepper
1 tablespoon dried oregano
juice of $^1/_2$ lemon
4–6 tablespoons olive oil

Soak the aubergine slices in salted water for about 20 minutes, then drain and pat dry with kitchen paper.

Cover a large baking tray or grill pan with aluminium foil and arrange the vegetables on it. Sprinkle with salt, pepper, the oregano and lemon juice and then drizzle the olive oil over the top. Place under a hot grill for about 10–12 minutes or until golden brown, then turn over and cook the other side for about 10 minutes.

*Emma Forbes*

# LEE'S HOTPOT

*Serves 4*

5 small new potatoes, chopped
2 carrots, chopped
50 g (2 oz) frozen peas
75 g (3 oz) pasta, such as fusilli
$1/_2$ onion, chopped
1 tablespoon vegetable oil
25 g (1 oz) butter or margarine
25 g (1 oz) plain flour
300 ml ($1/_2$ pint) hot milk
75 g (3 oz) cheese, grated
$1/_2$ teaspoon mustard
salt and freshly ground black pepper

Preheat the oven to 220°C (425°F, Gas Mark 7). Cook the potatoes, carrots and peas in boiling water until tender, then drain. In a separate pan, boil the pasta until just tender, then drain. Fry the onion in the oil until soft. Put all the vegetables and the pasta in an ovenproof dish.

Melt the butter or margarine in a pan, add the flour and stir for 1–2 minutes over a low heat. Gradually add the hot milk, stirring constantly, then remove from the heat and add the cheese, mustard, and salt and pepper to taste. Pour the sauce over the pasta and vegetables and cook in the oven for 10–15 minutes, until golden.

*Lee Donovan, London*

# POTATO PIZZAS

*Serves 2*

*Tasty mashed potato makes an unusual base for a pizza and children love it. I've used a classic cheese and tomato topping but the potatoes go well with almost any topping. For fun, you could decorate the pizzas to look like the face of a clown, with cucumber eyes, a cherry tomato nose and a strip of red pepper for the mouth.*

500 g (1 lb) potatoes, peeled and cut into chunks
25 g (1 oz) butter
2 spring onions, finely chopped, or 2 tablespoons chopped fresh chives
50 g (2 oz) plain flour
salt and freshly ground black pepper

*For the topping*
3 tomatoes, skinned and thinly sliced
75 g (3 oz) mozzarella cheese, sliced
1 tablespoon chopped fresh basil or $1/_2$ teaspoon dried oregano (optional)
25 g (1 oz) Cheddar cheese, grated

Preheat the oven to 200°C (400°F, Gas Mark 6). Boil the potatoes until tender, then drain and mash with the butter. Mix in the spring onions or chives and the flour and season with a little salt and pepper. Using floured hands, shape into 2 rounds about 13 cm (5 inch) in diameter and place on a greased baking sheet. Bake in the oven for about 20 minutes or until the edges become a little crispy.

Arrange the tomato slices in overlapping circles on top of the pizzas and top with the mozzarella. Sprinkle with the basil or oregano, if using, and scatter the Cheddar cheese on top. Place under a preheated grill until golden.

*Annabel Karmel*

In Russia the potato is known as the devil's apple.

# PUDDINGS

# AMAZINGLY HEALTHY ICE CREAM

*Serves 8*

*This is a relatively low-fat, low-sugar ice cream which all the children I know love. You can even make a good vegan version, and you could use carob instead of the chocolate if you prefer. It does freeze very hard and gets quite icy but children don't seem to mind at all. Sometimes I serve it with a hot chocolate sauce, which helps to melt it. Chocolate is a good source of iron.*

900 ml (1$^1/_2$ pints) low-fat milk or soya milk
125 g (4 oz) plain chocolate, broken into pieces
2 rounded tablespoons caster sugar
1 tablespoon custard powder
400 g (13 oz) can of evaporated milk (skimmed is fine) or soya cream

Put all but 4 tablespoons of the milk into a large saucepan with the chocolate and sugar and bring slowly to the boil. In a bowl, mix the custard powder to a paste with the rest of the milk. Add a little of the boiling milk to the custard mixture, stir, then pour the custard mixture into the pan of hot milk. Stir over the heat for 2–3 minutes until it has thickened a little, then remove from the heat. Add the evaporated milk or soya cream and whizz in a blender or food processor until smooth. Pour into a plastic container and leave to cool completely, then freeze until half set. Beat well, then freeze until firm. Remove this ice cream from the freezer about 40 minutes before you want to eat it. Serve with Quick Chocolate Sauce (see opposite) if you like.

*Rose Elliot*

Nurjahan lives in Bangladesh. She earns a living by making and selling ice creams. She pushes a small cart round the local area with her son who announces through a megaphone:
'Jony super ice cream made with banana, milk and butter.'

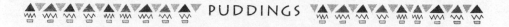 

# QUICK CHOCOLATE SAUCE

4 tablespoons cocoa powder
4 tablespoons sugar
150 ml ($^1/_4$ pint) water
15 g ($^1/_2$ oz) butter
2 tablespoons cream

Put the cocoa powder and sugar into a saucepan with the water, stir until smooth and bring to the boil. Remove from the heat, stir in the butter and cream, then serve.

*Rose Elliot*

# ORANGE SURPRISES

*This is a party pudding which children enjoy making, with a little help. You do need a really efficient freezer for chilling the oranges before serving.*

*Per person*
1 large, sweet orange
1 scoop of good-quality vanilla ice cream
a few hundreds and thousands (optional)

Slice a generously sized 'lid' off the orange; it should be cut deep enough to reveal the orange flesh and give a wide enough opening to scoop out the flesh. Then shave a little off the other end of the orange so that it will stand steady. Use a small sharp knife and a teaspoon to scoop the orange flesh out of both the 'lid' and the orange. Chop the flesh roughly, removing any pith and pips. Put the chopped flesh back into the orange, then top with the ice cream. Sprinkle with hundreds and thousands, if you like, and replace the 'lid'. Wrap the orange in clingfilm and freeze until required.

*Rose Elliot*

# ORANGE DELIGHT

*Serves 4*

*Oranges are full of good things but children often don't eat them because of the bother of peeling them. They usually enjoy this simple pudding, where the hard work has been done for them.*

6 large sweet juicy oranges, preferably navel oranges
a little clear honey
a few drops of orange flower water or rosewater (optional)

Wash one of the oranges and remove a few long slivers of peel – a zester, which you can buy quite cheaply, is best for this. Put the peel into a bowl, then, holding an orange over the bowl to catch the juice, and using a sharp knife and a sawing action, peel it as if you were peeling an apple and want to produce one long curl of peel. Aim to cut off the white pith as well as the peel. Cut the orange segments away from between the folds of transparent skin and put the segments into the bowl. Repeat with the remaining oranges. Sweeten the mixture by dissolving a little clear honey in the juice and add a few drops of orange flower water or rosewater if you like. Pour this over the orange segments, cover and chill until ready to serve.

*Rose Elliot*

Oxfam's Organic Forest Honey is made by wild bees, which collect nectar from the flowers of tall 'honey trees' in a vast forest in northwest Zambia. The hives are made out of hollow logs or cylinders of bark sewn together by the honey collectors, who suspend them high up in the trees. The honey is dark and has an intense flavour.

# BITTER CHOCOLATE MOUSSE

*Serves 4*

*Most French children are made to remain at the table all through the meal and, of course, they are expected to behave. This, as I remember, was quite an ordeal, especially when the 'grown-ups' talked about unexciting topics such as politics, religion, education, etc., and ignored us totally. This sweet made it all worthwhile – the price of patience!*

125 g (4 oz) best-quality plain chocolate
5 egg whites
40 g ($1\frac{1}{2}$ oz) caster sugar
2 egg yolks

Break the chocolate into small pieces and place them in a large bowl. Set it over a pan of hot water to melt, stirring from time to time. Whisk the egg whites until they form soft peaks, then add the caster sugar and continue to whisk until firmer peaks are formed. Stir the egg yolks into the warm melted chocolate. Briskly whisk one-third of the egg white into the chocolate mixture, then fold in the remaining egg white delicately.

Spoon the chocolate mousse into a large serving bowl or 4 individual dishes and refrigerate for at least 3 hours.

*Raymond Blanc*

Note: *There is a possible risk of salmonella from raw eggs. They should not be eaten by very young children and babies.*

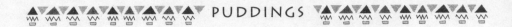 

# YOGURT AND PEAR PUDDING

*Serves 4*

*This can be made with other fruit, such as pineapple, apple or melon, instead of pears.*

4 tablespoons plain yogurt
2 pears, cored and finely chopped
2 teaspoons raisins
1 dessertspoon honey
1 teaspoon flavoured yogurt, or ground cinnamon or ginger

Put the plain yogurt in a mixing bowl and stir until smooth. Stir in the pears and raisins, then add the honey and flavoured yogurt or spice. Stir well and place in the fridge for about 10 minutes, then pour into 4 bowls and serve.

*Eleanor Jubb (aged 9), London*

# HASTY PUDDING

*Serves 4*

*The joy of this pudding is that children can add their own syrup and make patterns or write their names with it on the pudding, before finally stirring it in.*

25 g (1 oz) plain flour
600 ml (1 pint) milk
golden syrup, to taste

Mix the flour to a smooth paste with a little of the milk. Bring the rest of the milk to the boil and stir it into the cold mixture (not the other way round!). Return it to the pan and cook gently, stirring all the time, until it has a thick but pourable consistency. Pour into bowls and immediately add golden syrup.

*Susan Pomeroy, Harpenden, Hertfordshire*

# GRANGRAN'S CHOCOLATE PUDDING

*Serves 1–2*

*Grangran was my childish name for my grandmother and it stuck, both for her and this pudding, which she used to make when we went to visit her on Sundays. The quantities of flour and sugar can be altered according to taste. We always sprinkled more sugar on it before eating, to give a bit of crunchiness, but in the 1940s sugar was not considered to be bad for you!*

50 g (2 oz) plain flour
25 g (1 oz) cocoa powder
25–50 g (1–2 oz) sugar
600 ml (1 pint) milk

Mix the flour with the cocoa and sugar, then mix it to a smooth paste with a little of the milk. Make in the same way as Hasty Pudding (see page 135) but the consistency should be thicker and the pudding poured into a dish and allowed to cool before eating.

*Susan Pomeroy, Harpenden, Hertfordshire*

# HEALTHY BANANA SPLIT

*Serves 1*

1 banana
2 dessertspoons plain yogurt
a handful of raisins
a pinch of sugar (optional)

Peel the banana and cut it lengthways in half. Put it on a plate, sandwich it together with the yogurt and sprinkle the raisins on top with the sugar, if using.

*Eleanor Jubb (aged 9), London*

There are some weird and wonderful fruits out there. The durian might have the sweetest taste but it smells so foul that it is often banned by hotels and airlines. The mangosteen has such a fine flavour that Queen Victoria once offered a reward to anyone able to transport one back to England while still edible. The salak has a nut-brown surface which could be mistaken for snakeskin.

# SHRIKHAND

*Serves 4*

1.25 litres (2$\frac{1}{4}$ pints) yogurt
75 g (3 oz) icing sugar
flavouring of your choice, such as
$\frac{1}{4}$ teaspoon powdered saffron (or 5 saffron strands),
about 50 g (3 oz) crushed red berries or pistachio nuts,
a few drops of rosewater, or 1 teaspoon finely grated orange or lemon zest

Put the yogurt in a double layer of muslin, tie the ends together and hang it over a bowl to catch the drips. Leave in a cool place to drain overnight or for at least 5 hours.

Unwrap the yogurt and put it in another bowl. It should be very thick and reduced to half its original volume. Sift in the icing sugar, add the flavouring and beat with a whisk until smooth. Serve at room temperature or freeze the mixture to make a sort of ice cream.

*Aleksandar Obradovic, 'Food for Life', Serbia*

# BANANA SWEET

*Serves 4*

butter for frying
5 bananas, finely sliced
2 eggs
1 tablespoon plain flour
1 tablespoon caster sugar

Melt a little butter in a frying pan and gently cook the bananas for a few minutes. Whisk the eggs together in a bowl, then whisk in the flour. Pour the eggs over the bananas and cook gently, stirring, until they are scrambled. Arrange on serving plates and sprinkle with the sugar.

# ICED WHITE CHOCOLATE GATEAU

*Serves 4*

*I created this dish especially for children to prepare themselves and it does not require any cooking. A strawberry sauce goes very well with it. To make this, put fresh strawberries in a food processor with icing sugar to taste and process until smooth.*

150 g (5 oz) white chocolate, broken up
300 ml (¹/₂ pint) double cream
a selection of seasonal fruits, such as fresh berries or exotic fruits

*For the decoration*
75 g (3 oz) plain or milk chocolate
4 tablespoons whipping cream

Melt the white chocolate in a bowl set over a pan of hot water or in a microwave and stir until smooth. Add the cream a little at a time, stirring until combined. Pour into a 15 cm (6 inch) loose-bottomed cake tin and place in the freezer for approximately 30 minutes or until firm to the touch.

Meanwhile, prepare the fruit, removing any stalks and cutting large fruits into small chunks as necessary.

Remove the white chocolate gâteau from the tin, running a knife that has been dipped in hot water around the edges first to loosen it. Place it on a serving plate.

For the decoration, melt the plain or milk chocolate in the same way as the white chocolate. Draw a 15 cm (6 inch) circle on a piece of non-stick baking parchment, using the cake tin as a guide. Spread an even layer of melted chocolate in the marked circle and leave to set. Cut it into 8 triangles with a knife that has been dipped in hot water. Whip the cream until stiff and pipe 4 rosettes near the centre of the gâteau, then rest the tips of 2 chocolate triangles on top of each rosette so the triangles are tilted at an angle. Arrange the fruit around the edges to decorate.

*Dai Davies, Bryn Hotel, Llangollen, Clwyd*

# OAT GRIDDLE CAKES WITH APPLES AND PECANS

*Makes about 15*

125 g (4 oz) oatflakes
350 ml (12 fl oz) boiling water
1 egg
150 g (5 oz) plain flour
2 tablespoons baking powder
a pinch of salt
50 g (2 oz) granulated sugar
250 ml (8 fl oz) milk
50 g (2 oz) butter, melted
2–3 dessert apples, peeled, cored and finely chopped
50 g (2 oz) pecan nuts
sunflower oil for frying
maple syrup, to serve

Combine the oats and boiling water in a bowl and leave to stand for 5 minutes. Add the egg, flour, baking powder, salt and sugar and mix well, then stir in the milk, melted butter, apples and pecans.

Melt a little sunflower oil in a large non-stick frying pan over a medium heat. Add spoonfuls of the batter and cook for a few minutes until bubbles form on top, then gently flip them over and cook for another minute. Serve immediately, with maple syrup.

*Lucy Day, Horsham, West Sussex*

The sap of *Acer saccharum* was tapped by the native
Indians of North America, who used it as sugar.
Maple syrup is still popular, especially on
pancakes.

# QUICK CRUNCHY CRUMBLE

*Serves 4*

*This was invented when we decided to make a crumble with some leftover stewed apples only to discover we had run out of flour. Joe (then aged 7) had the idea of using Weetabix. It is a very quick and easy recipe for children to make, although they may need help preparing the fruit.*

*Instead of coconut you could use ground almonds or finely chopped nuts. If you are using apples, try adding $1/_2$ teaspoon ground cinnamon to the fruit.*

750 g (1$1/_2$ lb) fruit, such as apples, rhubarb or gooseberries
sugar, to taste

*For the crumble*
50 g (2 oz) butter or margarine
4 Weetabix
50 g (2 oz) light muscovado sugar
25 g (1 oz) desiccated coconut

Prepare the fruit as necessary and cook gently with a little water and sugar to taste. For the crumble, melt the butter or margarine in a pan. Crumble the Weetabix into a bowl and mix with the sugar and coconut. Pour the melted fat over the dry ingredients and mix thoroughly.

Put the warm stewed fruit in a heatproof dish, top with the crumble mixture and put under a medium grill for a few minutes to brown. Watch it carefully to make sure it does not burn.

*Julie Downs, Preston, Lancashire*

# FRUIT KEBABS

*Serves 4*

50 g (2 oz) butter
2 tablespoons honey
1 tablespoon lime juice
16 cherries, stoned
2 peaches, stoned and cut into cubes
2 slices of pineapple, cut into cubes
1 banana, sliced

Melt the butter in a pan and stir in the honey and lime juice. Boil for 1 minute to make a syrup, then remove the pan from the heat.

Arrange the fruit on kebab skewers and brush on one side with the syrup. Cook under a preheated grill, syrup-side up, for 3 minutes, then turn them over and brush the other side with syrup. Place them back under the grill and cook for another 3 minutes. Serve immediately.

The pineapple is made up of 100 fruits formed by a
spike of flowers.

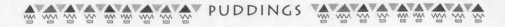
# APPLES IN A BLANKET

*Serves 6*

500 g (1 lb) shortcrust pastry
6 medium apples, peeled and cored
6 knobs of butter
6 tablespoons apricot jam
a little icing sugar

Preheat the oven to 200°C (400°F, Gas Mark 6). On a lightly floured surface, roll out the pastry thinly and cut it into six 15 cm (6 inch) squares, reserving the trimmings. Place an apple in the centre of each square and fill the cavity of each one with a knob of butter and a tablespoon of jam. Bring the corners of the pastry up over the top of each apple to enclose it completely. Re-roll the pastry trimmings and cut out 6 small circles. Cover the folded corners on top of each apple with a pastry circle.

Place the apples on a greased baking tray and bake for 40 minutes or until the apples are tender. Sprinkle with icing sugar and serve lukewarm.

# CHOCOLATE FROMAGE FRAIS

*Serves 6*

*You could flavour the fromage frais with orange or lemon juice instead of chocolate, adding honey or sugar to sweeten.*

200 g (7 oz) milk chocolate
750 g (1$^1/_2$ lb) fromage frais
extra fromage frais and chocolate, to decorate

Break up the chocolate and put it in a heatproof bowl. Stand the bowl over a pan of very hot water and stir the chocolate until it melts. Cool slightly and then fold the chocolate into the fromage frais.

Pour the mixture into serving dishes, top with extra fromage frais and grate extra chocolate over the top. Chill for 1 hour before serving.

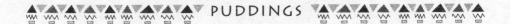 

# PUMPKIN PIE

*Serves 4–6*

*Fat orange pumpkins are sold in the autumn, and in America pumpkin pie is always a favourite at Thanksgiving Day dinner in November.*

250 g (8 oz) shortcrust pastry
1 small pumpkin, weighing about 1.15 kg ($2^3/_4$ lb)
3 eggs
300 ml ($^1/_2$ pint) double cream
$^1/_2$ teaspoon salt
150 g (5 oz) caster sugar
1 teaspoon ground ginger
1 teaspoon ground cinnamon
$^1/_2$ teaspoon ground nutmeg

Preheat the oven to 200°C (400°F, Gas Mark 6). Roll out the pastry on a lightly floured work surface and use to line a 23 cm (9 inch) pie dish. Cover with greaseproof paper, fill with baking beans or rice and bake for 10 minutes. Remove the paper and beans or rice and return to the oven for 5 minutes, until golden brown. Remove from the oven and reduce the heat to 190°C (375°F, Gas Mark 5).

Scoop the flesh out of the pumpkin, discarding the skin and seeds. Put the flesh in a pan, cover with water, and simmer for 25 minutes, until tender. Drain and leave to cool, then mash the pumpkin with a fork or purée it in a blender until it is perfectly smooth and free of lumps.

Beat the pumpkin with the eggs, cream, salt, sugar and spices. Pour into the pastry case, and bake for 40 minutes, until set. Serve with whipped cream, if liked.

# FERGUS'S PUDDING

*Serves 3–4*

*This is a huge favourite in my family and easily made by children. You could substitute a good crunchy muesli for the oats.*

about 50 g (2 oz) soft margarine
2 tablespoons soft brown sugar
about 4 tablespoons oatflakes

Melt the margarine in a pan and stir in the sugar. Cook for a few minutes until bubbly and thick, then stir in the porridge oats. Cool slightly, then serve with milk and sliced banana, ice cream, or fruit.

*Joanna King, Kirk Yetholm, Kelso*

Not only are oats a very nutritious grain which provides sustenance for nerves and tissues but oat husks are the raw material for 'furfural', a fluid used in making nylon.

# CAKES, BISCUITS & BREAD

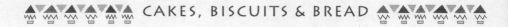 

# FAVOURITE GINGERBREAD MEN

### Makes 6

*All children love making gingerbread men but they often find the results disappointing to eat. I find this unconventional shortbread mixture, decorated with chocolate chips, the best – kids love it. It's easy to cut into shapes but young children may need help with the rolling out.*

150 g (6 oz) plain flour
$^{1}/_{2}$ teaspoon ground ginger
100 g (4 oz) softened butter or margarine
50 g (2 oz) caster sugar
milk chocolate chips, to decorate

Preheat the oven to 150°C (300°F, Gas Mark 2). Sift the flour and ginger on to a plate or a piece of greaseproof paper. Put the butter or margarine into a bowl with the sugar and beat with a wooden spoon until light and creamy – or whizz them in a food processor. Add the flour and ginger and mix to a firm dough either with your hands or in a food processor. Turn the dough on to a lightly floured board or a clean work surface and roll it out until it is about 5 mm ($^{1}/_{4}$ inch) thick. Cut into gingerbread men, or any other shapes you fancy, re-rolling the trimmings.

Put the gingerbread men on to a baking sheet and decorate them with chocolate chip eyes, mouths and buttons. Bake for about 45 minutes, or until they are crisp and dried through. Cool slightly, then transfer them to a wire tray. They will crisp further as they cool.

*Rose Elliot*

Allspice isn't all spices at all. It's a dark red-brown berry that belongs to the same family of plants as the myrtle, but it got its name because it has such a rich mixture of flavours.

# CARAMEL SQUARES

*Makes about 36*

*A version of 'millionaire's shortbread', these are always popular with children and nice to make for a treat.*

125 g (4 oz) butter or margarine
50 g (2 oz) caster sugar
175 g (6 oz) plain flour – wholemeal or a mixture of wholemeal and white

*For the filling*
125 g (4 oz) butter or margarine
50 g (2 oz) soft brown sugar
200 g (7 oz) can of condensed milk

*To finish*
100 g (3$^1/_2$ oz) milk chocolate, melted

Preheat the oven to 180°C (350°F, Gas Mark 4). Cream the butter or margarine and sugar together until light and fluffy, then stir in the flour. Turn on to a lightly floured surface and knead lightly, then roll out to a square. Press evenly into a greased shallow 23 cm (9 inch) square cake tin and prick all over with a fork. Bake for about 25 minutes, then leave to cool in the tin.

Meanwhile, put all the ingredients for the filling into a saucepan and heat gently, stirring, until dissolved. Bring slowly to the boil, then cook, stirring constantly, for 5–7 minutes. Leave to cool, then spread the filling over the base and leave to set. Spread with the melted chocolate. When it has set, cut the shortbread into small squares

*Rose Elliot*

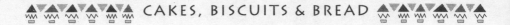 

# PARKIN

*Makes 12 slices*

*This recipe has always been a great favourite with my children. With the oatmeal, wholemeal flour and black treacle it's nutritious and it's easy to make. If you keep it for 2–7 days, wrapped in foil, it will get stickier. You can make a vegan version if you use golden syrup, margarine and soya milk.*

75 g (3 oz) dark brown sugar
125 g (4 oz) black treacle
125 g (4 oz) golden syrup or honey
125 g (4 oz) butter or margarine
175 ml (6 fl oz) milk
125 g (4 oz) wholemeal flour
125 g (4 oz) medium oatmeal
2 teaspoons ground ginger
2 teaspoons baking powder

Preheat the oven to 180°C (350°F, Gas Mark 4). Grease and line a 20 cm (8 inch) square cake tin. Put the sugar, treacle, syrup or honey and butter or margarine into a saucepan and heat gently to melt. Then remove from the heat, stir in the milk and leave on one side. Meanwhile, put the flour, oatmeal, ginger and baking powder into a large bowl and mix together. Make a well in the centre and pour in the melted mixture. Stir until everything is combined and then pour the mixture into the tin. Bake for 50–60 minutes, or until firm to the touch. Leave to cool in the tin, then cut into pieces.

*Rose Elliot*

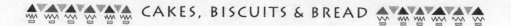 

# YOGURT CAKE

*Makes a 1 kg (2 lb) cake*

*Use the yogurt carton to measure the other ingredients for this quick and easy cake*

150 g (5 oz) carton of yogurt
1 carton of sunflower oil
2 cartons of caster sugar
3 cartons of self-raising flour
3 size-3 eggs
$1/_2$ teaspoon vanilla extract

Preheat the oven to 160°C (325°F, Gas Mark 3). Line a 1 kg (2 lb) loaf tin with baking parchment. Mix all the ingredients together very thoroughly until creamy. This can be done in a food processor. Put the mixture into the lined tin and smooth the top with a knife. Bake for $1^1/_4$–$1^1/_2$ hours, until the cake is firm on top and a skewer inserted in the centre comes out clean. Remove from the oven, leave in the tin for 5 minutes, then turn out on to a wire rack. Peel off the baking parchment and leave to cool.

*Tessa Brodetsky, Oxford Oxfam Group*

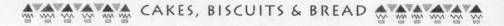
# CHOCOLATE CHIP COCONUT CAKE

*Makes a 1 kg (2 lb) cake*

*This recipe was concocted by my mother, based on the proportions of a fruit cake. It makes a great snack at teatime or just before bed.*

375 g (12 oz) self-raising flour
a pinch of salt
175 g (6 oz) butter or margarine
175 g (6 oz) caster sugar
75 g (3 oz) desiccated coconut
75–125 g (3–4 oz) chocolate chips
2 large eggs
about 175 ml (6 fl oz) milk

Preheat the oven to 180°C (350°F, Gas Mark 4). Grease and line a 1 kg (2 lb) loaf tin. Sift the flour and salt into a bowl and rub in the butter or margarine. Add the sugar, coconut and chocolate chips to the mixture and stir together.

In a separate bowl beat the eggs and milk together, then add to the dry ingredients. Beat until the mixture is fairly stiff with a dropping consistency. Place in the prepared tin, level the surface and bake for about $1\frac{1}{4}$ hours, or until a skewer inserted in the centre comes out clean. Cover the top of the cake if it becomes too brown. Turn out of the tin and leave on a wire rack to cool.

*Monica Stephen, Oxford*

The milk in unripe coconuts is a refreshing drink; the flesh can be eaten fresh or dried; the oil is used for cooking or soap; the husk or coir can be made into rope; the wood is light and flexible; the shells are used as utensils, or even to announce the arrival of a pantomime horse.

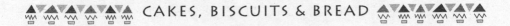 

# FRUIT LOAF

*Makes a 500 g (1 lb) loaf*

*This recipe first appeared on an All-Bran packet about 20 years ago and is absolutely delicious.*

1 heaped cup of All-Bran cereal
1 heaped cup of caster sugar
1 heaped cup of mixed dried fruit
1 cup of milk
1 heaped cup of self-raising flour

Put the All-Bran, sugar and dried fruit into a bowl and mix well together. Stir in the milk and leave to stand for 1 hour. Preheat the oven to 180°C (350°F, Gas Mark 4).

Sift the flour into the All-Bran mixture, stir well to combine and pour the mixture into a well-greased 500 g (1 lb) loaf tin. Bake for about $1\frac{1}{4}$–$1\frac{1}{2}$ hours, until well-risen and firm in the centre. Turn out on to a wire rack and leave to cool. To serve, cut into slices and spread with butter.

*Sally Stivers, Oxfam volunteer, Tewkesbury, Gloucestershire*

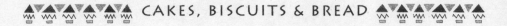 

# AUNT KATE'S CARROT CAKE

*Makes a 20 cm (8 inch) cake*

*A three-year-old wondered if carrot cake would make her hair curly: Aunt Kate wouldn't say. Try it and see!*

500 g (1 lb) carrots, cooked and mashed
4 eggs
400 g (14 oz) plain flour
2 teaspoons bicarbonate of soda
2 teaspoons baking powder
375 g (12 oz) caster sugar
350 ml (12 fl oz) vegetable oil
2 teaspoons ground cinnamon
150 g (5 oz) unsalted cashew nuts, chopped

Preheat the oven to 180°C (350°F, Gas Mark 4). Beat together the carrots and eggs. Add all the remaining ingredients and beat well, then pour into a greased and lined deep 20 cm (8 inch) round cake tin. Bake for $1^1/_2$–$1^3/_4$ hours or until a skewer inserted in the centre comes out clean. Cover towards the end of cooking if the cake is becoming too brown. Leave to cool in the tin for 10 minutes, then turn out on to a wire rack to cool completely.

# GRANDMA WHITESIDE'S CHADWICK CAKE

*Makes a 20 cm (8 inch) cake*

*I got this recipe from my Grandma, who inherited it from her mother – it is well over 100 years old. It always reminds me of afternoon visits after Sunday school, and is an excellent 'cut-and-come-again' cake. It is a good recipe for children who cannot eat eggs.*

175 g (6 oz) butter
200 g (7 oz) caster sugar
175 g (6 oz) currants
175 g (6 oz) sultanas
125 g (4 oz) candied peel
200 g (7 oz) ground rice
200 g (7 oz) self-raising flour
150 ml (¼ pint) milk
1 teaspoon bicarbonate of soda

Preheat the oven to 160°C (325°F, Gas Mark 3). Line a deep 20 cm (8 inch) round cake tin with a double layer of greaseproof paper. Cream the butter and sugar together until light and fluffy. Mix together the currants, sultanas, candied peel, ground rice and flour, then rub the creamed mixture into this mixture with your fingertips. Sprinkle the bicarbonate of soda over it and stir well, then bring the milk to the boil, pour it over the mixture and stir again.

Transfer to the prepared tin, cover with greaseproof paper and bake in the centre of the oven for 1–1½ hours, or until a skewer inserted in the centre comes out clean. Turn out on to a wire rack and leave to cool.

*Margaret Ellen Brookes, Blackpool, Lancashire*

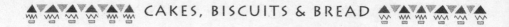 

# BANANA NUT BREAD

*Makes a 1 kg (2 lb) loaf*

275 g (9 oz) plain flour
2 teaspoons baking powder
$1/_2$ teaspoon salt
125 g (4 oz) butter or margarine
100 g ($3^1/_2$ oz) caster sugar
2 eggs, beaten
3 medium bananas, mashed
$1/_2$ teaspoon lemon essence (optional)
50 g (2 oz) nuts, chopped

Preheat the oven to 180°C (350°F, Gas Mark 4). Sift the flour, baking powder and salt into a bowl. In a separate bowl, cream together the butter or margarine and sugar, then add the beaten eggs and mix thoroughly. Stir in the dry ingredients alternately with the mashed bananas. Add the lemon essence, if using, and nuts and mix well. Pour into a greased 1 kg (2 lb) loaf tin and bake for 1 hour. Leave to cool in the tin for 10 minutes, then turn out on to a wire rack to cool completely.

*American Embassy*

'The bananas fruit all year, so there is always something coming up. There's also cassava and beans, so we survive that way.'

*Florence Elisa, of Kandegesho village, Tanzania, which was the first stop for Rwandan refugees and which has suffered a food shortage as a result*

# LAZY DAISY CAKE

*Makes a 20 cm (8 inch) cake*

2 eggs
175 g (6 oz) caster sugar
$1/_4$ teaspoon vanilla extract (optional)
125 g (4 oz) plain flour
$1/_4$ teaspoon salt
1 teaspoon baking powder
15 g ($1/_2$ oz) butter
125 ml (4 fl oz) milk

*For the topping*
40 g ($1^1/_2$ oz) butter, melted
5 tablespoons soft brown sugar
2 tablespoons cream
50 g (2 oz) walnuts, chopped

Preheat the oven to 200°C (400°F, Gas Mark 6). Beat the eggs well and then gradually beat in the sugar and the vanilla, if using.

Sift the flour, salt and baking powder into a bowl and fold into the egg mixture. Put the butter and milk in a pan and heat to boiling point, then add all at once to the mixture. Beat well. The batter will be thin but do not add any more flour. Pour into a buttered 20 cm (8 inch) round cake tin and bake for 30 minutes.

Meanwhile, put all the ingredients for the topping into a pan and simmer for a few minutes or until it leaves the sides of the pan. Remove the cake from the oven and, while still hot, spread with the topping. Return to the oven or place under a preheated grill until brown.

*Lady Curran*

# CHOCOLATE MUNCHIES

*Makes about 12*

*A version of an old favourite, which children can help to make. They are quite nutritious because of the cereal, seeds and dried fruit they contain.*

150 g (5 oz) good-quality plain or milk chocolate
50 g (2 oz) cornflakes
25 g (1 oz) sunflower seeds
25 g (1 oz) raisins

Break up the chocolate and put it in a bowl set over a pan of simmering water. Leave until the chocolate has melted, stirring occasionally, then remove the bowl from the pan. Add the cornflakes to the chocolate, crushing them with your fingers as you do so, then add the sunflower seeds and raisins and mix everything together. Put spoonfuls of the mixture into paper cake cases and leave to cool and set.

*Rose Elliot*

# WHOLEWHEAT GINGERBREAD

*Makes 12–15 slices*

125 g (4 oz) plain flour
a pinch of salt
1 teaspoon mixed spice
3 teaspoons ground ginger
125 g (4 oz) wholemeal flour
40 g (1½ oz) demerara sugar
40 g (1½ oz) sultanas
40 g (1½ oz) chopped mixed peel
125 g (4 oz) butter or margarine
125 g (4 oz) golden syrup
125 g (4 oz) black treacle
1 teaspoon bicarbonate of soda
150 ml (¼ pint) warm milk
1 egg, beaten
25 g (1 oz) split blanched almonds

Preheat the oven to 180°C (350°F, Gas Mark 4). Grease and line an oblong baking tin about 15 × 23 cm (6 × 9 inch). Sift the plain flour, salt and spices into a mixing bowl, then stir in the wholemeal flour, sugar, sultanas and mixed peel. Put the butter or margarine, golden syrup and treacle into a bowl, place over a pan of hot water and heat until melted, stirring occasionally. Add to the dry ingredients and beat well.

Dissolve the bicarbonate of soda in the warm milk and add the beaten egg. Pour this into the prepared mixture and beat well together to form a smooth batter. Pour into the prepared tin. Scatter the almonds over the top and bake in the centre of the oven for about 40–45 minutes or until well risen and springy to the touch. Cool in the tin, then turn out and cut into squares.

*Ruth Morgan*

# CHOCOLATE BROWNIES

*Makes 8–12*

*These brownies and the coffee cake opposite were made with Oxfam Fair Trade ingredients and distributed free as tasting samples to passing shoppers, together with recipe leaflets.*

125 g (4 oz) soft margarine, melted
2 eggs
2 tablespoons milk
250 g (8 oz) raw cane sugar
100 g (3½ oz) self-raising flour
1 teaspoon bicarbonate of soda
40 g (1½ oz) cocoa powder
50 g (2 oz) brazil nuts, chopped
50 g (2 oz) chocolate, melted (optional)

Preheat the oven to 180°C (350°F, Gas Mark 4). Beat together the melted margarine, eggs, milk and sugar. Sift the flour, bicarbonate of soda and cocoa into a separate bowl, then add to the other ingredients and mix well. Stir in the nuts and pour into a greased and lined 18 cm (7 inch) square cake tin. Bake in the oven for 30–40 minutes, or until a skewer inserted in the centre comes out clean. Cool in the tin and then drizzle with melted chocolate, if liked. Cut into squares to serve.

*Margaret Beech, Oxfam shop, Petergate, York*

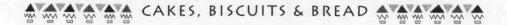 

# COFFEE CAKE

*Makes a 20 cm (8 inch) cake*

*This can be topped with coffee butter icing and sprinkled with chopped pecan nuts for a special occasion.*

175 g (6 oz) soft margarine
175 g (6 oz) raw cane sugar
3 eggs, beaten
175 g (6 oz) self-raising flour
1 dessertspoon instant coffee, dissolved in 1 tablespoon boiling water
50 g (2 oz) pecan nuts, chopped

Preheat the oven to 180°C (350°F, Gas Mark 4). Cream together the margarine and sugar until light and fluffy, then beat in the eggs a little at a time. Sift the flour and fold it into the mixture. Stir in the coffee and nuts and transfer the mixture to a greased and lined deep 20 cm (8 inch) round cake tin. Bake in the oven for 25–30 minutes or until well risen and golden brown. Turn out of the tin and leave to cool on a wire rack.

*Margaret Beech, Oxfam shop, Petergate, York*

*Hodja* is drunk in Ethiopia. It is made by boiling coffee leaves, a few coffee beans and salt in water and then adding milk. Farmers make it in the field wherever they are working and drink it under the shade of a tree.

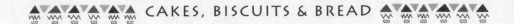 

# GRIDDLE CAKES

*Makes about 20*

250 g (8 oz) plain flour
1 teaspoon salt
1$^1/_2$ teaspoons baking powder
2 tablespoons sugar
1 egg, beaten
about 350 ml (12 fl oz) milk
1 teaspoon melted butter or margarine

Sift the flour, salt and baking powder into a bowl and stir in the sugar. Make a well in the centre and stir in the beaten egg and enough milk to make a thick batter. Add the melted butter or margarine and mix well. Drop tablespoonfuls of the mixture on to a hot greased griddle or a heavy frying pan and cook for 2–3 minutes per side, until golden brown. Serve with butter and jam or with maple syrup.

*Stirling Moss*

# COCONUT COOKIES

*Makes 12*

50 g (2 oz) plain flour
25 g (1 oz) desiccated coconut
25 g (1 oz) granulated sugar
50 g (2 oz) butter or margarine, diced
4 glacé cherries, each cut into 3, to decorate

Preheat the oven to 150°C (300°F, Gas Mark 2). Sift the flour into a bowl, add the coconut, sugar and butter or margarine and lightly mix in with your finger-tips. Knead well until completely blended together. Divide the mixture into 12 and roll into balls. Place them on a greased baking sheet and flatten slightly with your hand, then top each one with a piece of glacé cherry. Bake for about 15 minutes, then transfer to a wire rack to cool.

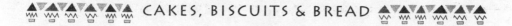
# HUFFSIE

*Makes a 1 kg (2 lb) loaf*

*This recipe was collected when we lived in Out Skerries in Shetland. Huffsie is really a generic Shetland term for a fruit loaf and this one is not only delicious but very easy to make. Since taking over its production my daughter, now aged 10, has had to write out the recipe umpteen times for visitors.*

1 cup of water
125 g (4 oz) margarine
1 cup of caster sugar
2 cups of sultanas
2 cups of self-raising flour
1 teaspoon bicarbonate of soda
2 eggs, beaten

Preheat the oven to 180°C (350°F, Gas Mark 4). Put the water, margarine, sugar and sultanas in a pan and boil for 10–15 minutes. Leave to cool. Sift the flour and bicarbonate of soda into a bowl, then add the sultana mixture and stir until thoroughly combined. Add the eggs and mix well. Pour into a well-greased and lined 1 kg (2 lb) loaf tin and bake for 40 minutes. Cover with foil and bake for a further 15–20 minutes, until a skewer inserted in the centre comes out clean. Turn out on to a wire rack to cool.

*Joanna King, Kirk Yetholm, Kelso*

# CARROT AND PINEAPPLE MUFFINS

*Serves 12–14*

*Muffins are just the right size for children and you can pack them full of nutritious ingredients. Serve plain or, for special occasions, ice with cream cheese icing and decorate to look like a cat, teddy bear, panda, etc.*

125 g (4 oz) plain flour
125 g (4 oz) wholemeal flour
1 teaspoon baking powder
$^3/_4$ teaspoon bicarbonate of soda
$1^1/_2$ teaspoons ground cinnamon
$^1/_2$ teaspoon salt
100 g ($3^1/_2$ oz) caster sugar
250 ml (8 fl oz) vegetable oil
2 eggs
125 g (4 oz) carrots, grated
250 g (8 oz) can of crushed pineapple, drained
40 g ($1^1/_2$ oz) pecans or walnuts, chopped
125 g (4 oz) raisins

Preheat the oven to 180°C (350°F, Gas Mark 4). Sift the flours, baking powder, bicarbonate of soda, cinnamon and salt into a bowl and mix well. In a separate bowl, beat together the sugar, oil and eggs until well blended. Add the grated carrots, crushed pineapple, nuts and raisins. Gradually add the flour mixture, beating just enough to combine all the ingredients.

Pour the batter into muffin trays lined with paper cases and bake for 25 minutes or until well risen and golden brown. Cool on a wire rack.

*Annabel Karmel*

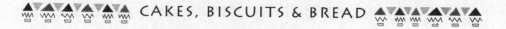 

# SWEET POTATO BUNS

*Makes about 15*

275 g (9 oz) sweet potato
50 g (2 oz) butter, melted
4 tablespoons milk
25 g (1 oz) granulated sugar
25 g (1 oz) sultanas
275 g (9 oz) self-raising flour
a pinch of salt
$1/_4$ teaspoon ground cinnamon

Preheat the oven to 220°C (425°F, Gas Mark 7). Peel the sweet potato and boil until soft, then drain thoroughly and mash. Mix with the melted butter and milk, then stir in the sugar and sultanas. Sift in the flour, salt and cinnamon and mix until well combined. Knead lightly to form a soft dough and then roll out on a lightly floured surface to about 5 mm ($1/_4$ inch) thick. Cut into rounds with an 8 cm (3 inch) cutter and place on a greased baking tray. Bake in the oven for 25–30 minutes, until golden brown, then transfer to a wire rack to cool.

# CHOCOLATE TREATS

*Makes about 18*

*You could add extra flavourings to these little cakes, such as chopped glacé cherries or raisins.*

125 g (4 oz) chocolate
50 g (2 oz) rice krispies

Break up the chocolate and melt it in a small basin set over a pan of hot water or in a microwave. Stir until smooth. Cool slightly and stir in the rice krispies, then place teaspoonfuls of the mixture on aluminium foil or greaseproof paper. Leave to set.

*Anthea M. Spurling, Sittingbourne, Kent*

# QUICK SHORTBREAD

*Makes about 20*

250 g (8 oz) plain flour
100 g (3$\frac{1}{2}$ oz) custard powder or cornflour
(custard powder gives a nice colour)
100 g (3$\frac{1}{2}$ oz) icing sugar
250 g (8 oz) butter

Preheat the oven to 180°C (350°F, Gas Mark 4). Sift the flour, custard powder or cornflour and icing sugar into a bowl, then rub in the butter to form a stiff dough. Shape into a roll about 5 cm (2 inch) in diameter and cut into slices 5 mm ($\frac{1}{4}$ inch) thick. Place on a greased baking sheet and press lightly with the back of a fork to give a ridged effect. Bake for about 15 minutes; do not let the biscuits brown. Transfer to a wire rack to cool.

*Stefanie Bryl, Oxfam volunteer, Nottingham*

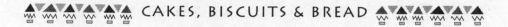 

# SUZIE'S FLOP

*Makes about 24*

*These simple biscuits are quick and easy to make and they keep well in an airtight tin or in the freezer. For a special treat, cover with melted chocolate while still hot, then let the chocolate cool a little and mark into squares.*

200 g (7 oz) block margarine
50 g (2 oz) golden syrup
125 g (4 oz) oats (a combination of rolled and jumbo)
4 tablespoons plain flour
50 g (2 oz) granulated sugar
3 tablespoons oat bran

Preheat the oven to 180°C (350°F, Gas Mark 4). Melt the fat and syrup in a large saucepan but do not let it sizzle. Remove the pan from the heat, add all the remaining ingredients and combine thoroughly. Press into a greased and lined Swiss roll tin and bake in the oven for 15–20 minutes, until golden brown. Remove from the oven, mark into squares with a knife and leave to cool in the tin, placed on a wire rack.

*Suzie Scaife, Lower Gresham, Norfolk*

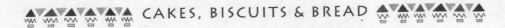
# CHOCOLATE CHIP COOKIES

*Makes about 36*

*Glacé cherries, nuts or dried fruit could be substituted for the chocolate, with mixed spice or almond essence added as a flavouring.*

175 g (6 oz) block margarine
175 g (6 oz) caster sugar
2 eggs
1 teaspoon vanilla extract
375 g (12 oz) self-raising flour
200 g (7 oz) chocolate chips

Preheat the oven to 180°C (350°F, Gas Mark 4). Cream together the margarine and sugar until light and fluffy, then gradually beat in the eggs and vanilla extract. Stir in the flour and chocolate chips. Place teaspoonfuls of the mixture on greased baking sheets (they only spread a little). Bake for about 10 minutes, until golden, then transfer to a wire rack to cool.

*Anthea M. Spurling, Sittingbourne, Kent*

Cocoa and chocolate come from the cacao tree. Originally from the American tropics, most cocoa is now produced in West Africa. Rather strangely, the flowers and pods grow from the main trunk and branches. The cocoa beans are scooped out of the pod and fermented – in a heap covered by banana leaves on small estates or, most often, in special sweat boxes – then they are dried for export. It is the importing countries that shell, roast and grind the beans to make cocoa.

# POPPY SEED WHEATGERM OATMEAL LOAF

*Makes a 1 kg (2 lb) loaf or two 500 g (1 lb) loaves or 12 rolls*

*This bread is fun to make, especially for children, and is jolly tasty. My children particularly enjoy shaping the dough into rolls – hedgehog rolls are popular.*

2 scant teaspoons dried yeast
1 teaspoon sugar or honey
450 ml ($^3/_4$ pint) lukewarm water or milk and water mixed
750 g ($1^1/_2$ lb) unbleached strong white flour
40 g ($1^1/_2$ oz) wheatgerm
40 g ($1^1/_2$ oz) medium oatmeal
2 teaspoons poppy seeds
$1^1/_2$ teaspoons salt
2 tablespoons olive oil

Mix the yeast and sugar or honey with 150 ml ($^1/_4$ pint) of the warm liquid. Leave for about 10 minutes, until frothy.

Place the flour, wheatgerm, oatmeal, poppy seeds and salt in a large bowl and lightly combine by lifting your fingers through the mixture. Add the olive oil and activated yeast, plus the remaining liquid, and mix together to form a smooth, pliable dough. (If it is too wet, add a little more flour; if too dry, a little more lukewarm liquid.) Knead for 10 minutes on a lightly floured work surface, then replace in the bowl and cover with a plastic carrier bag. Leave at room temperature for 2 hours or until doubled in size. If more convenient, you can also leave it overnight in the fridge to rise.

Knead lightly for 2 minutes, giving an initial firm pinch to expel all the gases that have accumulated and redistributing the air bubbles throughout the dough. Place in a greased 1 kg (2 lb) loaf tin or two 500 g (1 lb) tins, or shape into 12 rolls, and place on a greased baking sheet. Cover with a polythene bag and leave in a warm place for $1^1/_2$ hours or until doubled in size. Meanwhile preheat the oven to 220°C (425°F, Gas Mark 7).

Place the bread in the centre of the oven for 15 minutes, then reduce the temperature to 200°C (400°F, Gas Mark 6) and bake for a further 15 minutes. Rolls will only take 20 minutes. Remove the bread from the tin, invert on to the oven shelf and bake for a final 15 minutes (or 5 minutes for rolls). To test if baked, tap the bottom of the loaf; if it sounds hollow, it is done. Leave to cool in a draught-free place.

*Suzie Scaife, Lower Gresham, Norfolk*

# MIXED GRAIN WHOLEMEAL LOAF

*Makes a 1 kg (2 lb) loaf or two 500 g (1 lb) loaves or 12 rolls*

*A wonderful nutty-flavoured loaf which children love.*

2 scant teaspoons dried yeast
1 teaspoon sugar, honey, treacle or molasses
450 ml ($^3/_4$ pint) lukewarm water, or milk and water mixed
250 g (8 oz) strong wholemeal flour
500 g (1 lb) unbleached strong white flour
40 g ($1^1/_2$ oz) bran
40 g ($1^1/_2$ oz) medium oatmeal
2 teaspoons sesame seeds
$1^1/_2$ teaspoons salt
2 tablespoons olive oil

Follow the method for Poppy Seed Wheatgerm Oatmeal Loaf (see page 171).

*Suzie Scaife, Lower Gresham, Norfolk*

The Egyptians were probably the first people to
grind wheat into flour to make bread. Archaeologists
have found evidence of bakeries there dating
back to 2000 BC

# SWEETS & DRINKS

# FUDGE

*Makes about 1 kg (2 lb)*

*While we all agree that it's not good for children to have too much sugar, everyone needs a treat sometimes and this fudge recipe is a winner.*

125 g (4 oz) butter
400 g (13 oz) can of condensed milk
500 g (1 lb) caster sugar
a few drops of vanilla extract

Line a 20 cm (8 inch) square cake tin with non-stick paper. Put the butter in a large saucepan and melt over a gentle heat, then add the condensed milk and sugar and continue to heat gently until the sugar has dissolved. Raise the heat a little and boil, stirring frequently, until the mixture will form a soft ball when a little of it is dropped into a cup of cold water. Don't worry if brown specks rise to the surface of the mixture as it cooks – these will disperse to create a caramel colour – but don't let it burn on the bottom.

Remove the pan from the heat and put it into a bowl of cold water to cool it down quickly. Add the vanilla and beat the mixture as it cools. It will become grainy and begin to set; at this point pour it quickly into the tin. Mark the fudge into squares when cool, then cut it when it is completely cold.

*Rose Elliot*

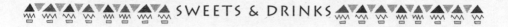 

# ROCKY ROAD BANANAS

*Makes 4*

*This is a great recipe if you have too many ripe bananas. Once frozen, the bananas will keep for weeks – unless they are eaten immediately as in my house! If you prefer you can slice the bananas to make bite-sized treats. As a variation, try mixing a few tablespoons of carob powder into the honey and then roll them in coconut, dates or nuts – or all three!*

4 ripe bananas
runny honey for coating
50–125 g (2–4 oz) Brazil nuts, coarsely ground

Simply peel the bananas and skewer them on kebab or ice lolly sticks. Roll them in honey and then in the nuts. Put on a freezerproof plate and freeze until hard. Eat straight from the stick.

*Leslie Kenton*

Contrary to popular belief, bananas don't grow on trees. The *musaceae* are actually a family of giant, tree-like herbs which grow 3–9 metres (10–30 feet) high. A whole bunch of bananas can weigh 36 kg (80 lb)

# FONDANTS

*Makes 250 g (8 oz)*

*These are easy sweets for children to make. They can be flavoured with peppermint or vanilla extract, fruit flavouring or a few drops of strong black coffee, and suitable colourings can be added, if liked.*

250 g (8 oz) icing sugar
$1^1/_2$ tablespoons evaporated milk
a few drops of flavouring (see above)

Sift the icing sugar into a bowl, add the evaporated milk and mix well to form a dough. Stir in flavouring of your choice to taste, then roll the mixture into little balls. Press into sweet moulds or petit four cases and leave until firm. They only keep for a few days.

*Variations:* Coat the balls with desiccated coconut, grated chocolate or finely chopped nuts. Press half walnuts or almonds into the balls of fondant, or stuff the fondant into stoned dates.

*Lucy Day, Horsham, West Sussex*

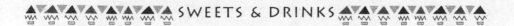 

# SIMPLY WONDERFULS

*Makes about 40*

*These are so easy to assemble that children can turn out a successful batch for grown-up treats.*

125 g (4 oz) unsalted butter
50 g (2 oz) icing sugar
200 g (7 oz) dried milk powder (not granules)
1 teaspoon milk or cream (optional)
a few drops of flavouring, such as vanilla or almond extract,
lemon or lime juice or 2 tablespoons finely chopped nuts,
glacé cherries or dried apricots

Cream the butter and icing sugar together in a mixing bowl until light and fluffy. Using your hands, work in the milk powder, adding the milk or cream if necessary to make a medium-soft fondant. Add the flavouring and continue to work until well blended. (All this can be done in a food processor.)

Roll the fondant into small balls. You can also roll it around whole nuts, sandwich it between nut halves or dip the balls in melted chocolate. Place in little paper sweet cases and store in the fridge in a well-sealed container for up to 4 days. Serve chilled or at room temperature.

*Aleksandar Obradovic, 'Food for Life', Serbia*

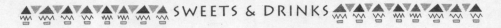 

# CHOCOLATE TRUFFLE CHRISTMAS PUDDINGS

*Makes 30*

*These truffles are extremely versatile. You could add some chopped raisins soaked in brandy or glacé cherries soaked in sherry, or omit the alcohol altogether for young children. You could also dip the truffles in melted chocolate (white, milk or plain) or roll them in coconut, cocoa powder or chocolate vermicelli.*

125 g (4 oz) plain chocolate
75 g (3 oz) cake or biscuit crumbs
75 g (3 oz) icing sugar, sifted
75 g (3 oz) ground almonds
2 tablespoons brandy
4 tablespoons double cream
fondant (see opposite)

Melt the chocolate in a bowl set over a pan of simmering water or in a microwave. Put the crumbs, icing sugar, almonds and brandy into a bowl and stir in the melted chocolate, then add the cream and stir to combine. Refrigerate for at least 1 hour.

Take small teaspoonfuls of the mixture and roll them into balls, then top with a splodge of fondant. Decorate with a dot of red fondant for a holly berry and two green fondant motifs either side of the red dot for the leaves. Place in petit four cases. These truffles will keep for 2–3 weeks in an airtight container; put sheets of greaseproof paper between the layers.

*Suzie Scaife, Lower Gresham, Norfolk*

# EASY FONDANT

*This is an excellent cake covering for special-occasion cakes and it takes a food colouring very well. Keep wrapped in a polythene bag if not using immediately and knead it a little before use again.*

500 g (1 lb) icing sugar
1 egg white
2 teaspoons golden syrup or liquid glucose

Sift the sugar into a bowl, add the egg white and syrup or glucose and knead until well combined and smooth. This can be done in a food processor.

*Suzie Scaife, Lower Gresham, Norfolk*

# STRAWBERRY ALMOND SHAKE

*Serves 1*

*This creamy drink is full of nutrients, almost a light meal in itself.*

4 strawberries
200 ml (7 fl oz) soya milk
25 g (1 oz) ground almonds
honey to taste (optional)

Wash and hull the strawberries, then put them in the freezer and leave until really cold and solid (alternatively you could use bought frozen strawberries). Chill the soya milk and almonds in the fridge. When you are ready to make the drink, put the strawberries, soya milk and almonds in a blender or food processor and whizz to a creamy consistency. Sweeten to taste with a dash of honey, if you like, then pour into a tall glass to serve.

*Rose Elliot*

# BANANA PUNCH

*Serves 2*

2 bananas
300 ml (¹/₂ pint) milk
3 tablespoons yogurt
1 tablespoon clear honey
pinch of nutmeg

Peel and chop the bananas. Put them in a blender with the milk, yogurt, honey and nutmeg and blend until smooth (if too thick, add a little more milk). Pour into glasses and serve immediately.

'Bananas are my whole livelihood. The farm is my own but we work it as a family.'

*Edme Celestin, a banana farmer in St Lucia*

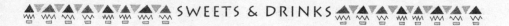 

# ELDERFLOWER CORDIAL

*Makes 300 ml ($^1/_2$ pint)*

*Elderflower cordial is now available in delicatessens and large supermarkets but it is very quick – and much cheaper – to make your own. Even in large towns, most people will be able to find an elder tree or bush nearby and in the early summer months they are laden with creamy blossoms. Choose a tree away from traffic-laden main roads, if possible. Pick the flowers when they are at their best and use them immediately.*

*This is an easy recipe for children to make themselves.*

3 heads of elderflower
300 ml ($^1/_2$ pint) water
75 g (3 oz) caster sugar
zest and juice of $^1/_2$ lemon

Shake the elderflower heads to get rid of any dust or tiny insects but do not wash them. Put the water, sugar and lemon zest and juice into a pan and heat gently, stirring, until the sugar has completely dissolved. Add the elderflowers and bring to the boil, then remove from the heat, cover and leave to cool. Strain through a fine sieve or a piece of muslin and pour into a bottle.

The cordial will keep in the fridge for weeks. It makes a refreshing drink diluted with fizzy water and served with ice and a slice of lemon. It can also be used neat to flavour a fruit salad or compote.

*Jane Middleton*

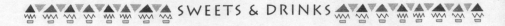 

# LEMONADE

*Makes about 2 litres (3¹/₂ pints)*

*This lemonade will keep for months in the refrigerator although it usually gets drunk very quickly as it is such a lovely refreshing drink.*

4 lemons
750 g (1¹/₂ lb) granulated sugar
1.2 litres (2 pints) boiling water
25 g (1 oz) citric acid

Pare the zest from the lemons then squeeze out the juice. Put the zest, plus pips and pith, into a large bowl. Add the sugar, boiling water and citric acid. Stir well, cover and leave until quite cold. Strain and bottle. Serve 1 tablespoon stirred into a glass of water, or to taste.

*Lucy Day, Horsham, West Sussex*

How do you like your cup of tea? In India, where it is known as *chai*, all the ingredients are boiled up together and people drink it very sweet and milky. The nomads of West Africa prefer sweet mint tea served in glasses.

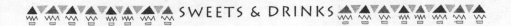 

# LASSI

*Serves 4*

*Lassi, made from yogurt, is a common accompaniment to curry meals in India but as it is so easy to make you can drink it any time as a change from soft drinks. For a savoury version, flavour it with a little salt instead of sugar, or you can serve it plain.*

300 ml ($1/_2$ pint) chilled yogurt
600 ml (1 pint) cold water
juice of $1/_2$ lemon
2 teaspoons sugar

Simply whisk all the ingredients together or liquidize them in a blender until frothy, then pour into glasses.

# LIMEADE

*Serves 4*

5 limes, unpeeled and roughly cut up into chunks (remove pips)
sugar, to taste
about 900 ml ($1^1/_2$ pints) water

Put the lime chunks into a blender with sugar and water to taste and process briefly, until the fruit is quite finely chopped. Do not overprocess or it will taste bitter. Strain and adjust the amount of sugar if necessary. Add ice and serve.

# INDEX

# ACKNOWLEDGEMENTS

Oxfam, Rose Elliot and the Publishers would like to thank Oxfam's supporters, volunteers and staff for contributing so actively to this collection. Thanks are also due for kind permission to reproduce the following recipes from other publications:

SNACKS, SALADS AND SOUPS

Carrot and Radish Salad (*The Food Book*, Troth Wells)
Fruity Vegetable Salad (*Good Housekeeping Cooking for Vegetarian Children*, Janet Smith and Fiona Hunter)
Miso Soup (*A Taste of Japan*, Jenny Ridgwell)

CHEESE AND EGGS

Stuffed Eggs (*The Food Book*, Troth Wells)
Omelette with Beansprouts (*The Food Book*, Troth Wells)
Rolled Omelette with Peas (*A Taste of Japan*, Jenny Ridgwell)

SAVOURY PASTRY DISHES

Vegetable Samosas (*Good Housekeeping Kids' Cookbook*, Janet Smith)
Borek (*Kids Around the World*)

RICE AND GRAINS

Vegetable Couscous (*Good Housekeeping Cooking for Vegetarian Children*, Janet Smith and Fiona Hunter)
Gnocchi (*Good Housekeeping Cooking for Vegetarian Children*, Janet Smith and Fiona Hunter)
Millet and Lentil Bake (*The Food Book*, Troth Wells)

PULSES

Aubergine Gratin (*Good Housekeeping Cooking for Vegetarian Children*, Janet Smith and Fiona Hunter)
Lentil and Cheese Bake (*The Food Book*, Troth Wells)
Spiced Beans in Coconut Milk (*The World in Your Kitchen*, Troth Wells)
Black-eyed Bean Stew (*The World in Your Kitchen*, Troth Wells)
Mung Beans in Coconut Milk (*The World in Your Kitchen*, Troth Wells)
Beans and Corn (*The World in Your Kitchen*, Troth Wells)
Dal with Coconut (*The World in Your Kitchen*, Troth Wells)
Irio (*Little Cooks*, Unicef)
Refritos with Guacamole and Salsa (*Kids Around the World*)
Red Bean and Rice Salad (*Caribbean Cookery Cards*, pub. by Tamarind)

VEGETABLES AND NUTS
Potato Cakes with Peanut Sauce (*The World in Your Kitchen*, Troth Wells)
Walnut Balls (*The Food Book*, Troth Wells)
Pumpkin au Gratin (*Little Cooks*, Unicef)
Corn Fritters (*Kids Around the World*)

PUDDINGS
Bitter Chocolate Mousse (*Cooking for Friends*, Raymond Blanc, Headline)
Banana Sweet (*Little Cooks*, Unicef)
Fruit Kebabs (*Little Cooks*, Unicef)
Apples in a Blanket (*Little Cooks*, Unicef)
Pumpkin Pie (*Kids Around the World*)
Chocolate Fromage Frais (*Kids Around the World*)

CAKES, BISCUITS AND BREAD
Aunt Kate's Carrot Cake (*A Taste for Justice*)
Banana Nut Bread (*Chefs Galore*)
Griddle Cakes (*Chefs Galore*)
Lazy Daisy Cake (*Chefs Galore*)
Wholewheat Gingerbread (*Chefs Galore*)
Sweet Potato Buns (*Easy Caribbean Cooking*, pub. by Tamarind)

DRINKS AND SWEETS
Banana Punch (*Easy Caribbean Cooking*, pub. by Tamarind)
Lassi (*The Food Book*, Troth Wells)
Limeade (*The World in Your Kitchen*, Troth Wells)